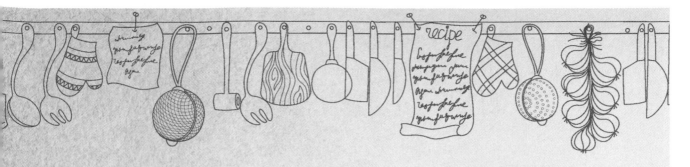

Val's Kitchen

VALERIE O'CONNOR is a cook, food writer and photographer; her column inches can be found in many national newspapers. She teaches classes in traditional cooking skills and has worked in professional kitchens from Brussels to Malaysia. She is a qualified Organic Horticulturalist and blogs about her food adventures at www.valskitchen.com. Her first book, *Bread on the Table*, is also published by The O'Brien Press.

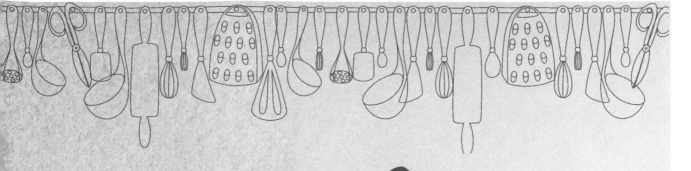

Val's Kitchen

REAL FOOD, REAL EASY

WRITTEN AND PHOTOGRAPHED BY

Valerie O'Connor

THE O'BRIEN PRESS
DUBLIN

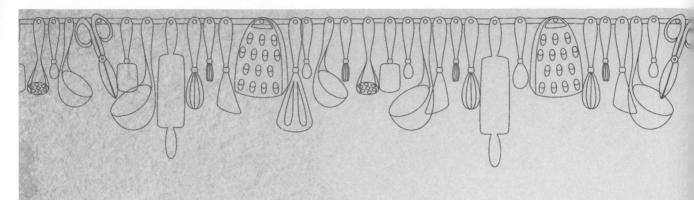

First published 2016 by
The O'Brien Press Ltd,
12 Terenure Road East, Rathgar,
Dublin 6, D06 HD27. Ireland.
Tel: +353 1 4923333; Fax: +353 1 4922777
E-mail: books@obrien.ie.
Website: www.obrien.ie

ISBN: 978-1-84717-721-6

Printed and bound in Poland by Białostockie Zakłady Graficzne S.A.
The paper in this book is produced using pulp from managed forests.

Published in:

DUBLIN
UNESCO
City of Literature

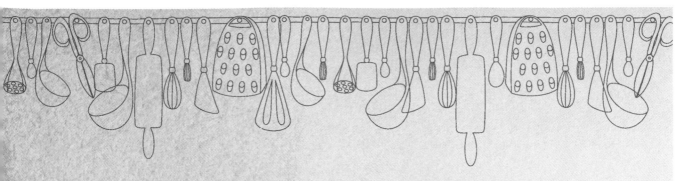

Dedication

Thank you to you, the reader, for buying my book. I hope you love the recipes

and make them over and over again,

Valerie

Acknowledgements

Thanks to my boys, Leon and Saoirse – great eaters – to my brother, Chris, and to

my mum and dad for their love of food. To Melissa Gillan on Inis Mór (Oileáin

Árann) for introducing me to fermenting, and to my pals Nicola, Karen, Linda,

Laura, Dee and Maggie, always there – x.

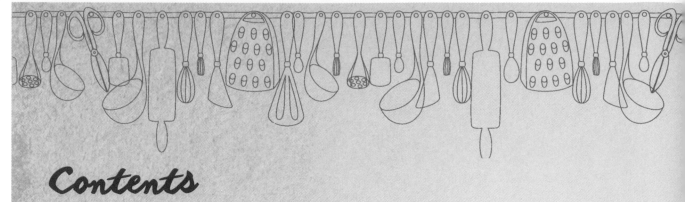

Contents

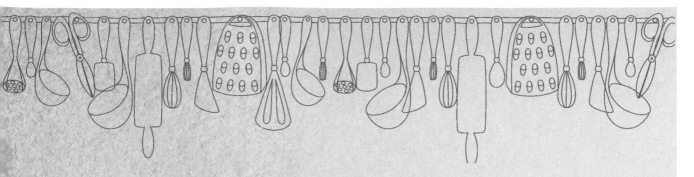

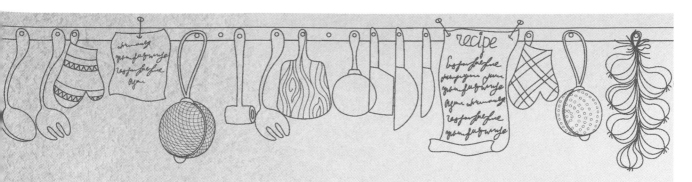

An Unremarkable Beginning

When we were growing up, my parents seemed like polar opposites when it came to food; my mother was a real traditionalist who loved offal, skirts and kidneys, packet and tripe, ox tongue and made them for herself on a regular basis while we three kids made gagging faces and pinched our noses in disgust. Mum would enjoy the fat from a juicy lamb chop, while I carved it all off, already under the influence of the 'low fat' advertising we were being bombarded with through our TV screens. Dad, on the other hand, had spent much of his early career at sea as a radio officer in the merchant navy where he developed a taste for the exotic, so we grew up eating more curries, Italian food and exotic 'foreign' food than was usual.

I used to compare our dinners to my friends; I envied them for eating 'cool' stuff like crispy pancakes and instant noodles, fish fingers and frozen chips. I hated the fact that we always had fresh fish and chips made from actual potatoes instead of from the 'chipper', but now, I know I was lucky.

At fourteen I announced that I was a vegetarian (because it was cool). My mother quite rightly told me I could do my own cooking and so I did. This was in the day before broccoli or garlic, never mind lentils, aubergines and different cheeses. My staple diet became potato and tomato 'pie' (layers of potatoes, tomatoes, onions and breadcrumbs) and tins of tuna (because in 1980s Ireland fish was considered a vegetable). My heart wasn't in it, though and I craved the gorgeous beef curries, lasagnes and stews my mother was cooking. My brother relished tormenting me at dinner times as he sliced into

his chicken breast 'Mmmm, chicken!' he'd slaver as he cut through the plump white meat, coated in the delicious creamy sauce that Mum had lovingly prepared and simmered all morning for us. My eyes would be out on stalks as I filled up on another potato pie instead.

As an eighteen-year-old in London on my first summer away from home and college looking for a job, the vegetarianess began to crack. I wandered around with a friend in Victoria Station, down on luck and money and she announced that she was going for a burger. I sat in front of her as she chomped happily on her meat patty, with a wholemeal bun as concession. I got up, got one and never looked back. I stopped by the butchers shop and supermarket on my way home and made my mother's lasagne that night. I realised then how much I'd been influenced by both my parents and how much I'd learned from them in the kitchen.

Now that I'm a mother of two teens I know only too well that time spent in the kitchen is unavoidable if you want to nourish yourself and your family – but it needn't be a chore! A pot of stock takes little effort or money and can be frozen; loaves of sourdough bread can be baked just once a week. Fermenting vegetables means you always have a jar or two to dip into when you don't feel like preparing fresh ones, so a meal can easily be a slab of sourdough and a good cheese, some sauerkraut with a bowl of soup. Our parents and grandparents were right all along as they prepared nutritious meals, made from the cheaper cuts with plenty of vegetables and good grains like barley and

oats. How right we were in Ireland to be dousing our potatoes in butter, making them more digestible, and knocking back glasses of pure pro-biotic buttermilk. Porridge soaked overnight, then served smothered in cream and honey, black pudding, grass-fed meat – we had it all!

Rethink your kitchen, ditch the processed foods and your life will improve in ways you can't imagine. Grow a few herbs and salads and get connected to where your food comes from. It's cheap, it's easy, it's fun and it's fulfilling.

Valerie O'Connor 2015

The Big Breakfast

Breakfast is the most important meal of the day; what better motivation to get out of bed than the thought of some delicious Bircher muesli in summer or creamy porridge in winter, or a plate of scrambled eggs on sourdough toast with some fresh juice, or yogurt, cheese or pâté? At weekends my sons and I might loosen things up a bit with pancakes, cheesy muffins, a 'fry' or all of the above. Personally, eggs are always my number-one choice for the first meal of the day; I don't have space to keep chickens so instead I buy the best, freshest eggs I can, mostly from our local co-op or the Limerick Milk Market.

Another thing I love about breakfast foods is that they easily convert into brunch food. Sunday late breakfast with friends is a great social occasion and something we did a lot in the years we lived in Germany; boiled eggs, cheese, salamis, smoked salmon, quark, fruit and all manner of different breads meant lazy hours nibbling on this and that.

While no one has hours to spend munching away in a leisurely fashion of a Monday morning, having a few handy staples in will make sure you have a good start to the day. Skipping breakfast leads to poor concentration and a likelihood to reach for sugary, fatty, processed foods, so stock up and treat yourself well with these suggestions.

The Breakfast Pantry

Eggs vary in quality, so it's worth finding a good supplier and stocking up every week. Eggs are one of the most important foods in your kitchen. They contain so many vitamins and nutrients and are very filling; you'll consume less junk if you eat more of them. There's a huge range of delicious egg dishes for breakfast, from boiled or fried eggs, to scrambled eggs, omelettes and beyond. Try different types of egg; duck eggs make the best cakes and are great fried in coconut oil as it gives the whites really crispy edges.

Oats are among the oldest and most important grains in the Irish diet; they grow well here in our wet climate and can be used in so many ways. Like our parents and grandparents did for their breakfast porridge, it's best to soak oats overnight, ideally with a little whey, and cook them with a little salt.

Honey is nature's sweet treat and medicine cabinet all in one. As well as being perfect drizzled on your breakfast porridge or swirled into yoghurt, it's a great energy booster and builds a strong immune system, chasing away colds and easing sore throats. Hot milk with real honey is a soothing and delicious bedtime drink; a spoonful of honey an hour before bedtime is said to help you burn fat in your sleep as well as promoting a great night's kip. If you know any beekeepers, make friends with them, local honey is like gold and will help you with any allergies you might have.

Nuts can also feature in a healthy breakfast (see Nutola page 22) are the perfect snack food and bursting with proteins and vitamins.

The thought of *coffee* in the morning is one of the best motivators to get me out of bed. Although the world is full of expensive coffee machines, I like to make my coffee in a basic Bodum plunger or French press – cheap and cheerful and I can buy whatever coffee I want. Though when stuck, I have made coffee in the foot of a pair of tights! The best coffee I've ever tasted was in Vietnam where they make the black stuff strong enough to stand a spoon up in. At tiny roadside cafes you will see rows of metal coffee sitting over glasses with dark coffee slowly dripping onto sweetened condensed milk. This is then stirred up and enjoyed hot or poured over ice when it has the texture and flavour of Kahlua. The coffee pot in the photo is a traditional Greek one I saw in a woman's house where we were doing some soda bread baking for a book launch.

It can be hard on your digestion to start the day with a cup of the black stuff so try and have a mug of boiled water or hot water with lemon juice first. This is great for getting your digestive juices flowing and is less of a shock to your system than cold water. Drinking mugs of hot water throughout the day will help rid your body of toxins, promoting a strong liver and clear skin.

Real Bread is something I love to have for breakfast – my favourite staple being a delicious sourdough that I make all the time; happily, my lads love it too. I love my easy oat bread too, especially topped with butter and sliced bananas. When my first book, *Bread on the Table*, was published I was often met by people who told me they would love to eat bread, but it just didn't suit them; bread was taking a hammering and it wasn't fair! I always reply that that stuff in plastic wrappers in supermarkets isn't bread. Real bread is made from unbleached flour – wheat, rye, oats, spelt – that hasn't been chemically treated or sprayed with pesticides. It's made with water, salt and yeast or sourdough. Find yourself a real baker, and never let them go, or get my first book, which shows you how to make real, healthy bread.

Butter, my favourite topping for my breakfast toast, has finally been given its 'get out of jail free' card, making me sigh with relief and happiness. Living in our rainy country means we have the lushest pasture which makes the best milk and the best butter. Butter contains healthy saturated fats, lowers your risk of heart attack and has no connection to obesity. So then next time you see the rain fall, just thank nature for giving us the best butter (and grass-fed beef) in the world.

Bulletproof Coffee

I didn't make up this drink's name – it sounds much too macho and high-powered for me. But trust me, it's like the silkiest, smoothest and most indulgent latte you'll ever get your lips around! If you're someone who doesn't like breakfast, this qualifies as both eating and drinking coffee – you'll be full until lunchtime. If you choose to use salted butter, it still tastes good, but you will need to add extra honey for balance.

Serves one

Ingredients

Coffee, fresh ground and ideally organic
2 tbsp butter, preferably unsalted (Kerrygold or Glenstal will do nicely)
2 tbsp coconut oil
1-2 tbsp honey

You will need a blender

Method

1. Make your coffee in your usual way – I use a French press; nice, strong coffee is good for this.
2. Warm the blender jug with boiled water from the kettle, swirl it around and pour it out.
3. Pour in enough coffee for one – about 300ml – add the butter, coconut oil and honey and blitz until it's all nice and frothy.
4. Pour into a nice, tall latte glass and enjoy every, gorgeous, creamy sip with a slice of the yogurt cake (p 103) and sit smugly at your table telling yourself you're having coffee and cake for breakfast – and it's good for you!

Crunchy Granola

Since when did getting your oats in become so sexy? Chowing down on a bowl or tub of granola is tasty, satisfying and yummy. You can make yours with organic jumbo oat flakes or spelt flakes, which are widely available from health food shops. Making granola requires a bit of attention in the kitchen, but is so worth the effort and gives your whole household a healthy and filling breakfast and snack to nibble on.

Ingredients

500g rolled oats, or jumbo oat flakes, or spelt flakes
120g butter or extra-virgin coconut oil
6 tbsp runny honey
500g mixed nuts, brazil nuts, hazelnuts and almonds, roughly chopped
200g mixed seeds (sunflower and pumpkin are best)
300-400g mixed fruit (like raisins, cranberries, chopped apricots) or
200g dried banana, apple, coconut and strawberry chips
1 tsp cinnamon
1 tsp ground ginger
1/2 tsp sea salt
Preheat the oven to 170C/350F/Gas3

Makes enough to fill a big tub. Store in an airtight container.

Method

1. In a small pot, melt the butter or coconut oil with the honey and spices.
2. Mix everything else, except the fruit, together in a large bowl and pour the melty mixture over it. Stir everything together with two large spoons, or your hands, and spread it out over two large roasting trays (at least 20 x 30cm).
3. Pop the trays in the oven for 20 minutes, then take them out and stir everything around to ensure it cooks evenly.
4. Bake for a further 20-30 minutes and take out when it's all a nice golden brown colour.
5. Tip the lot into a large mixing bowl or basin and allow it to cool (if you leave it to cool on the baking tray it will stick!), occasionally mixing it or breaking up large clusters with a large spoon
6. Mix in the dried fruit and your granola is ready to munch!
7. Once you get in the habit of making this you can get experimental with your own flavour combinations. Why not try banana and coconut, strawberry and apple, pineapple and mango?

Nutola!

Making your own cereals and snacks is a great way of breaking a habit of eating the sugary, processed versions. When you find yourself hungry at work, or after a workout, having something with an instant energy boost that will stave off cravings is essential. This Nutola is highly addictive and totally delicious. It takes a bit of effort to make, so make a decent batch and you'll be sorted for a couple of weeks. You can keep this as a tub of snack food in your bag, sprinkle it on yogurt or other cereals, have it in some milk, or any way at all. Cayenne pepper might seem a bit bizarre, but it's very subtle. I added it firstly out of curiosity as I don't like things that are really sweet and it gives just enough of a curious kick.

Ingredients

2 bags (approx 100g per bag) mixed nuts (I get mine from Dunnes as I don't like cashews and there aren't any in the mix, it's mostly Brazils, almonds and hazelnuts, but use any nuts you like except for peanuts, which are hard to digest)
2 bags (approx 100g per bag) of mixed seeds or 200g each pumpkin and sunflower seeds
350g dried mixed fruit, raisins, sultanas, cranberries
50g extra virgin coconut oil/butter
4 tbsp honey
1 tsp cinnamon
1/2 tsp cayenne pepper
Preheat the oven to 170C/320F/Gas3

Method

1. In a small pot melt the oil or butter, honey and spices.
2. On a large chopping board use a large knife or cleaver to roughly chop the nuts into chunky pieces. (If you come up with a way to do this that doesn't result in nuts flying all over the kitchen, please let me know.) Go slowly, you make less mess.
3. Tip the chopped nuts and the seeds into a large roasting tray, 30 x 20cm, and mix them around.
4. Pour over the oil and honey mixture and mix it all around using two spoons or your hands until everything is coated.
5. Pop the tray into the centre of the oven and cook for 20 minutes, then take the tray out and stir everything around, put it back in. Do this again in 20 minutes and then take the tray out after a total or 50-60 minutes. It can burn very easily and it doesn't taste good when this happens so no sneaking off to watch *Fair City*.
6. When you take the tray out of the oven, tip everything into a large bowl; if you leave it to cool in the tray it will all stick to the bottom of the tray and your life will be hell.
7. While the mix is cooling give it the odd stir to shake it up and stop huge clusters forming.
8. Add in the fruit and mix it all around again, *et voila*, your Nutola is ready. It keeps well in a sealed container for a few weeks.

Bircher Muesli Two Ways

Bircher Muesli is named after Maximilian Bircher-Benner, a Swiss doctor and nutritionist, who developed it for patients at his Zurich sanatorium at the turn of the last century. It was used as an alkaline meal (it has no refined carbohydrates and the amount of oats used is negligible). Grating an apple into it makes it more interesting to eat, but you still get all of the fibre. This apple recipe is the classic recipe, but I've included a variant as well. It goes without saying, so I'll say it, that the better the ingredients you use, the better the results. Making this with in-season Irish apples, and adding good organic yogurt and honey will give you a flavourful bowl of lightness and energy. It's surprisingly addictive and if you like porridge in winter you can easily swap to this in summer.

Serves one

Ingredients

1tbsp rolled oats

3-4 tbsp water

1 delicious apple, the juicier the better (you can tell if an apple is juicy by flicking the back of your fingernail at it, if it sounds high pitched, it's firm and full of juice, if it sounds dull, then it's dry and mealy)

1 tbsp runny honey

2-4 tbsp natural yogurt

Method

1. The night before, mix the oats with the water and leave them in the fridge.

2. In the morning, drain the oats by squeezing them gently to get the water out.

3. Grate the apple into a bowl, pour the yogurt onto the apple, add the drained oats, mix everything up in the bowl and drizzle over the runny honey.

Serves two

Ingredients

50g rolled organic oats

200g natural yogurt

A little water

4 tbsp frozen mixed berries

2 tbsp flax seeds

2 tbsp runny honey

2 tbsp dried cranberries

2 tbsp pumpkin seeds

Method

1. This more commonly seen 'Bircher muesli' has no apple in it and is mostly oat based, making it good to store in the fridge for a couple of days. You can bring it to work as a light but filling snack. Mix everything together, keeping back a few berries and seeds for topping; add a little water if it seems too thick.

2. Divide the mixture between two bowls or pots and leave overnight in the fridge.

3. Sprinkle on some extra pumpkin seeds and cranberries for crunch and serve!

Oat or Spelt Porridge

You can make this porridge from spelt flakes (available from health food shops) or from organic oatmeal. Whichever way you make it, you'll have a gluten-free breakfast; oats are naturally gluten free, but cannot be labelled so, as they're transported in trucks that also transport wheat so there is some cross-contamination. If you are not coeliac, you have no gluten to fear from oats. As with all grains, it's better to soak these overnight; they make a much creamier porridge this way. I add some flaxseeds to the mix for improved digestion and they all but disappear. The best porridge oats make the best porridge, Macroom is yummy and I am also a big fan of using pinhead oatmeal for an amazing, nutty texture. You can add dried fruit to the mix if you like, or cinnamon, but this is a good base to get started on.

Serves 2 people
Ingredients
60g porridge, pinhead oats or spelt flakes
1/2 pint water
1 tbsp flaxseed
Tiny pinch of salt
Runny honey, to taste
Blueberries/bananas/other berries, for topping
Fresh pouring cream

Method
1. Mix the oats, water, seeds and salt together and leave to soak overnight.
2. Bring everything to a boil in a heavy-bottomed pot and reduce the heat to a gentle simmer and stir regularly until you have a consistency you like; about 10 to 15 minutes should do it.
3. Dish up the porridge and top with anything you fancy, my favourite combos are bananas and honey or blueberries and honey. You just have to finish it off with a good drizzle of cream and maybe a sprinkling of cinnamon! Yum.

A Few Good Eggs!

I can't imagine a world without eggs; as a child I used to believe that the 'Our Father' (a prayer we recited, em, religiously) ended with the mantra 'And world without eggs, Amen'. I couldn't imagine why God would be so cruel as to eliminate eggs from the world! No scrambled eggs, or runny boiled eggs with soldiers, or shiny fried eggs, crispy in coconut oil or silky in butter – well, it's not worth thinking about!

You can eat eggs any time of day, but they really are the perfect breakfast food; they're so tasty on their own that there's no need to do anything fancy to them, you can prepare them really quickly. You've heard the expression 'couldn't boil an egg'? Well plenty of people can't, so here are a few basics to ensure you can have your eggs and eat them.

Boiled Egg

A recipe for a boiled egg, really? Yes. It's something that people struggle with and everybody has their own way of doing this.

When I lived in Germany I discovered the *Eier Stecher*, roughly translated as the 'egg-hole maker'. This wondrous gizmo makes a tiny hole into the bottom of the egg, allowing the trapped air at the bottom of the membrane to escape, that's what makes them crack. If you can't get an egg-holer, you can make a hole in the bottom of the egg with a tiny knife or a pin. Once you've made the hole, use a spoon to pop the egg into a small pot of boiling water. When it starts to leap around in the pot cook it for 3 minutes for a medium egg and 4 minutes for a large one.

Scrambled eggs

I don't use milk in scrambled eggs and I don't see the need, without milk they will be glossy and rich in texture.

Ingredients
2 eggs per person
1 large knob butter
Parsley or chives or chive flowers, to garnish
Salt and pepper

Method
1. Use a heavy pan, cast iron ideally, to make your scrambled eggs. Heat up the pan and let a good-sized knob of butter heat up and run around to coat the bottom of the pan.
2. Crack the eggs straight into the pan and, using a wooden or rubber spoon, quickly break up the yolks and slightly whisk them in the pan, now leave them cook a little, turn them over gently and as soon as they look glossy, turn off the heat. Sprinkle over a little sea salt and black pepper and sprinkle on a few tiny chive flowers if you have them or parsley if you don't, or both, or neither!
3. When I make smoked salmon with scrambled eggs I just drape a couple of slices of good-quality salmon over the cooked eggs; the heat from the eggs is enough to warm the salmon through.

Poached Eggs

I don't bother with tornados in pots of water and vinegar. There are easier ways to poach an egg! The most important thing is the freshness of the egg – a less-fresh egg white will spill all over the place in the pan.

Get a deep frying pan (big enough to fit an egg-lifter so that you can get the egg out) and fill it with water. When the water is boiling, break your egg into a cup. Take the pan off the heat to stop the bubbles and slide the egg into the water. Return the pan to the heat and let the egg cook for 3-4 minutes, depending on the size of the egg – when the yolk starts to become a tiny bit opaque, it's cooked. Fish it out with the egg lifter, or a large slotted spoon, holding it over a tea-towel or kitchen paper so the water can run off and you don't get soggy toast!

The Veg-Out Omelette

One of my favourite breakfasts came from the Wild Onion Café in Limerick where the feisty Ruth would hold court every Saturday policing customers who had the audacity to walk in and expect a table in their tiny, bustling diner. Ruth stood, notebook in hand, marshalling the hungry crowd who stood in line waiting for a table. Their breakfasts were the stuff of legend; this was my favourite so I'm attempting to re-create it in homage to Bob and Ruth who have now moved their business to a small bakery on the Ennis Road.

Serves 1
Ingredients
A mixture of broccoli, peppers, mushrooms and onions or anything that will griddle well, about a handful of each
Cheddar cheese, to garnish
A few slices of a medium chilli
3 fresh eggs
Butter, for frying the omelette
Olive oil, for cooking the veg

Method
1. Heat up a large griddle pan and slice the veg into even thicknesses so they will all cook in a similar time. Drizzle on a little olive oil and throw on the veg. Let them get a bit burnt at the edges, then turn them over; this gives a great flavour. They should be done in about 6-8 minutes. Remove to a warm plate.
2. Meanwhile make your omelette. You will need a decent sized pan here, cast iron pan or ceramic, ideally. Heat the pan and melt a good sized knob of butter to evenly coat the bottom. Quickly whisk your eggs in a bowl with a little salt and pepper and pour the mixture onto the frying pan.
3. Let this bubble up and don't disturb it. When it starts to look cooked around the edges carefully slide the veggies onto one side of the eggs. Leave them to settle, then pop on your chilli and cheese and let it melt. Then flip the eggy side over onto the veg and slide the omelette out of the pan onto a warm plate.
Variation: you can just as easily fill an omelette with some steamed kale and top it with a few slices of fried chorizo, yummy and no need for cheese.

Perfect Pancakes

Elvis Pancakes

The banana has to be nature's ultimate fast food. It comes in its own wrapper, can be eaten anywhere, is naturally sweet and filling and is full of potassium, making it the perfect thing to eat just before you go to sleep. It's a carbohydrate, but it's not refined, so you can stuff your face! Bananas are ready to eat when they have brown or black spots on them and not before. These pancakes are made from two of my favourite ingredients – peanut butter and banana – also much loved by the King who would approve of them being fried in butter.

Makes 6-8 small pancakes
Ingredients
2 large ripe bananas
2 large eggs
1 heaped tbsp peanut butter or almond butter
Butter or coconut oil for frying
Extra banana for slicing and serving
Honey for drizzling

Method
1. Toss everything into a blender and switch it on, it will miraculously turn to a creamy batter in about 30 seconds.
2. Heat a frying pan, melt some butter or coconut oil and pour on some batter. Allow it to cook until a lot of bubbles appear on the surface, then flip it over. Cook on the other side and keep this and all the ensuing pancakes warm in the oven, until all the batter is used up.
3. Slice more fresh banana or other fruit on top and drizzle with honey.

Oatmeal Pancakes

I find there's always some porridge left over in the mornings, and this is a great way of using it up. Simply blitz everything in the food processor for an easy, delicious and hearty pancake batter. This is a great way to get oatmeal into family members who wouldn't touch porridge, understandable as these are delicious, all buttery and fried. Make this batter the night before if you can.

Makes 10-12 pancakes
Ingredients
100g oat flour (you can make this by blitzing 100g regular oats in a blender) or use plain flour here
100g leftover cold porridge
2 tsp baking powder
1/2 tsp salt
250ml milk or buttermilk
1 tbsp molasses (unsulphured)
2 eggs
Extra butter or coconut oil for the pan
Preheat the oven to 130C/250F/Gas1 to keep the pancakes warm.

Method

1. Throw everything into the blender and blitz until you have a smooth batter. If you prefer the idea of more texture in your pancakes, then mix everything by hand in a large bowl.

2. You can use this immediately if you wish or keep it overnight in the fridge.

3. Heat up 1 tbsp butter on a heavy frying pan and pour on enough batter to make a pancake of about 10-12 cm round. When bubbles appear on the surface, flip the pancake over and add a little more butter to the pan. Flip on to a plate and keep them warm in the oven while you make the rest.

4. I love these with a simple fruit coulis I make by heating up some frozen mixed berries (available from most supermarkets) with a couple of squeezes of runny honey. Simply warm it in the pan until bubbling for a couple of minutes. Pour this over the pancakes with a little scoop of Greek yogurt.

Juices

All these recipes serve one and the method for each juice is the same, just juice everything! My kids love apple and pineapple juice with lime or just apple and carrot juice. My number one favourite is the 'ABC', apple, carrot and beetroot; its gorgeous colour is enough to make you feel good.

'ABC'

Easy squeezy, this is a juice I have most days.

1 apple
1 medium beetroot
1-2 carrots
1 lemon

Apple and Pineapple

A winning combo that kids love as it gets so frothy in the juicer. You can tell if a pineapple is ripe by pulling at its leaves, if the central ones come out easily, it's nice and sweet.

2 sweet apples
1 large chunk of really sweet pineapple
Squeeze of lime juice

Apple, carrot and ginger

A winter immune-system booster with the added power of ginger to help eliminate colds and stuffy noses.

2 sweet apples
1 carrot, scraped clean
1 thumb sized piece of fresh ginger, scraped clean

Supergreen power juice

You will need a juicer that can handle greens and leaves for any green juice

A handful each of kale and broccoli florets
1 stick celery
1 sweet apple
A few sprigs of chickweed, nettle tops or dandelion greens, when in season

Smoothies

Smoothies have become as normal as fizzy drinks in recent years; you can pick them up from the fridge in any supermarket or corner shop. But making your own smoothies is cheaper and you have full control over what goes into them, not to mention that you can drink them straight away to benefit from all the goodness. If there is one advantage in drinking/eating smoothies over juices it's that smoothies use the whole fruit so you get the fibre as well as the juice. Bags of frozen berries from the supermarket will be your best friend here and you can choose to juice apples or use a good quality cloudy apple juice. One main misunderstanding is that smoothies always contain dairy; they don't have to – a banana will make a thicker, sweeter smoothie than one with yogurt, just make sure to use really ripe bananas.

Mixed Berry Smoothie

Makes 2 servings
Ingredients
100g frozen mixed berries (I rarely measure these, but about a cupful)
200ml apple juice, cloudy (clear is usually made from concentrate)
1 or 2 ripe bananas, depending on size
A squeeze of honey
1. Blitz everything together in the blender, pour into glasses and drink. You might have lumpy bits, but who cares?

Banana Milkshake

Homer Simpson says 'Bananas are an excellent source of potassium' and he's right! They're also a great morning-after-the-night-before cure, so much better than a big fry up. If you can't resist the call of a plate of bacon and pudding, at least get one of these into you first.

My favourite smoothie is a simple banana milkshake made with – yes, you guessed – ripe bananas and some fresh milk. All these banana recipes serve one.

Ingredients
200ml fresh, full-fat milk
1- 2 ripe bananas
(For a filling variation, simply add some oats that you've soaked in water overnight to the blender.)

Method
1. Just pop them into the blender and blitz until smooth, it's almost as good as an ice cream one, if not better.

Jerusalem Smoothie

Too delicious for words, the ultimate instant meal if you're in a hurry. Filling and delicious, more like lunch than breakfast.

Ingredients

1-2 ripe bananas

2 tbsp smooth peanut butter

1 tbsp tahini

250ml fresh full-fat milk

Method

1. Blitz until smooth. Just yummy!

Coconut, pineapple and banana smoothie

Coconut water is the fastest and most effective thing to rehydrate you and it also gets rid of headaches in a flash as I accidentally discovered one Halloween when I drank the water from a coconut and noticed, ten minutes later, that a murderous headache I'd been carrying around was suddenly gone.

Ingredients

200ml coconut water

1-2 ripe bananas

1/4 fresh pineapple, chopped

Method

1. Throw everything into the blender and blitz until smooth. This totally tropical bombshell will have you bouncing around in no time.

Super seaweed smoothie

This smoothie is inspired by the amazing Dr Prannie Rhatigan, a GP and seaweed specialist. Seaweed has so many uses and a range of vitamins and nutrients beyond measure. You don't need to go trawling the shores for this free food as Spanish Point Sea Vegetables have developed their family business to produce a range of more user-friendly seaweed from dried packets of kombu, sea spaghetti and carrigeen, to sprinkles versions of the different veggies and all the way to powdered dilisk. The more different types of greens and fruits you use the better so one small piece of seaweed or one nettle is better than a whole bunch.

Ingredients

A handful of dandelion leaves, nettle, chickweed, mint
A few leaves of spinach, kale, broccoli
Half a teaspoon of seaweed sprinkles:
nori, kombu, dilisk OR if you have fresh or dried seaweed use one 15cm piece of Alaria soaked overnight
A large chunk of pineapple for sweetness
A very ripe banana for thickness
250ml water
1 tbsp honey

Method

1. Go outside with your scissors and cut a variety of wild greens – dandelion leaves, nettle, chickweed, mint. Put all ingredients in the blender and blitz everything together until it has a good smooth consistency. Drink and enjoy a nutrition powerhouse from the sky and the sea.

Light Bites

Welsh Rarebit

Another home classic from my mum. We used to have this for 'tea' back when people had a smaller meal in the evening rather than a big dinner. Use the strongest cheddar cheese you can get and enjoy the indulgent luxury of this much, much more than just cheese on toast dish.

Serves 2
Ingredients
25g butter
25g flour
250ml whole milk
100g strong cheddar cheese, grated
½ tsp English mustard
Drizzle Worcestershire sauce
Good bread for toast, ideally sourdough, 2 large or 4 smaller slices, cut nice and thick
Black pepper, to taste

Method
1. In a heavy-based saucepan, melt the butter over a medium heat and add in the flour, stir this and cook for at least 2 minutes.
2. Slowly pour in the milk while stirring the sauce constantly. Don't worry if it appears lumpy, the lumps will cook out.
3. Throw in the cheese and let it melt slowly, stirring gently, then add in the mustard and maybe a grind of black pepper.
4. Preheat your grill and toast some good bread, preferably sourdough (you can toast it in the toaster too but you'll need the grill anyway).
5. Get a large plate each and put your toast onto it, butter if you want, and pour over the cheese sauce, drizzle with a little Worcestershire sauce.
6. Place the plate under the hot grill and let it cook until black bubbles appear on the surface.
7. Your delicious, posh cheese on toast is now ready to eat. Enjoy with a big mug of tea.

Variation:
You can easily use the cheese sauce to make up a pasta bake; just mix it through some cooked pasta with maybe a few cooked bacon bits and have it for dinner.

Vegetable Chips and Kale Crisps

Celeriac is a yummy vegetable that, like a lot of veggies, belies its unattractive appearance. It can be baked, mashed or turned into gorgeous creamy soups with none of the starchiness of the humble spud and a lot more flavour. You can also use parsnips, sweet potatoes, or beetroot but the beetroot won't get as crispy.

Serves 4 as a side dish
Ingredients
1 celeriac, peeled and cut into regular-sized chips or sliced into circles (or 3-4 parsnips or beetroots, sliced)
3 tbsp coconut oil/olive oil/lard/ beef dripping/goose or duck fat
Sea salt, to sprinkle
Preheat the oven to 200C/400F/Gas 6

Method
1. Put a steamer over a pot of boiling water and pop the veggies on to cook for about 5 minutes. Tip them out onto a clean tea towel to let some of the moisture evaporate.
2. Pour about 3 tbsp of oil or fat into a roasting tray and heat in the oven.
3. Tip the veggie chips into the fat and turn them over to coat. Sprinkle over a little sea salt. Roast the chips in the hot oven for 30 minutes, turning them halfway through cooking until they look crispy.

Variation
1. Sweet potato chips don't need to be pre-steamed as they cook much faster. Sprinkling these with a little cayenne pepper or cumin works well, and coconut oil or olive oil suits them best.

Kale Crisps
Crisps made from cabbage! They really taste great, and are delicious with beer. Use curly kale, *cavolo nero*, or any variety that you fancy. You can get some great ones from most supermarkets or farmers markets (especially when in season from July to October), or better still, grow your own.

Serves 4 as a snack
Ingredients
1 head kale or 250g bag, washed and dried with the ribs removed
2 tbsp olive oil
1 tsp sea salt
Preheat the oven to 180C/350F/Gas4

Method

1. Cut the kale into pieces of about 5cm long.

2. In a large bowl drizzle over some olive oil, just enough to barely cover the kale and give it a quick massage to make sure it's evenly coated.

3. Get 1 or 2 roasting trays, depending on how much kale you are cooking. Spread the kale out on the trays. It shouldn't overlap. Sprinkle over the sea salt.

4. Bake the kale crisps in the oven for 20 minutes until they are crispy and crunchy and that's it. Enjoy this salty, guilt-free snack.

Hummus

Hummus is easy to buy, but also easy to make – and you can make it just how you like it. I love this version as it's made without olive oil, you just pour some on at the end. It's super creamy and very rich due to the high tahini count. The toasted cumin gives it another dimension too.

Makes lots for you and to share
Ingredients
500g tin cooked chickpeas, preferably organic
140g tahini
3 cloves garlic, chopped
Juice of 1 lemon/3 to 4 tbsp, depending on how zingy you like it
½ tsp cumin seeds, toasted lightly on a dry frying pan and ground
60ml ice-cold water
½ tsp sea salt
Grind or two black pepper
Olive oil and some whole chickpeas to serve

Method
1. Throw everything, except the cold water, olive oil and salt and pepper, into a food processor or sturdy blender, blitz until things are getting mushy, slowly pour in the water and keep it blending until you have a silky smooth texture.
2. Spoon it out into a bowl and mix in your salt and pepper to taste.
3. Smooth over the top and pour on some olive oil and add a few chickpeas for appearances, sprinkle over a little parsley or coriander.

Variation
For a wild pink version of hummus, just add a chopped cooked beet to the blender. Follow the recipe as above, leaving out the tahini.

Wilted Kale and Avocado Salad

This is a salad that can be left in the fridge for a couple of days and actually gets better over time. Massaging the kale reduces its tough chewiness and results in a raw food salad bursting with fresh flavours and nutrients. Use this recipe as a guideline and add or subtract your favourite ingredients as you like.

Ingredients
Serves 2
250g kale with ribs removed, any variety, washed and torn into pieces
1 tbsp sea salt
2 tbsp soy sauce or tamari
2 tbsp crunchy peanut butter
1 tbsp sesame seeds, toasted
1 or 2 avocados
Cayenne pepper, to serve
1 lemon
Olive oil

Method
1. In a large bowl, massage the kale with the sea salt for about ten minutes and then leave it at room temperature for at least half an hour to soften.
2. Meanwhile, mix the soy sauce or tamari with the peanut butter until it's well combined, pour this over the kale and toss well to coat the leaves.
3. Toast the sesame seeds: heat a dry frying pan on a medium heat and add a thin layer of seeds to the pan. Let them toast for a minute or two and shake the pan around to make sure they don't burn, once they have all changed colour slightly, turn them out onto a cold plate. You can store these in a jar to use as you like.
4. To serve, divide the kale between plates, slice an avocado and arrange it on top, squeeze over some lemon juice and a drizzle of olive oil with a little sprinkle of cayenne pepper and tuck in.
5. The kale mix will keep for a couple of days, covered in the fridge.

Some Great Salads

Rainbow Salad

This 'salad in a jar' looks so appetising. It's made by layering everything and packing it tightly into a glass jar with a lid.

Serves 1
Ingredients
200g/7oz tin cooked chickpeas
¼ small red onion, diced
Handful red cabbage, shredded
1 carrot, shredded
Handful rocket/mizuna/baby spinach leaves
100g/ 4oz cooked chorizo pieces

Dressing
Juice one lime
1 tbsp thai fish sauce
2 tbsp light olive oil
1 tsp sesame oil

Method

1. Pour the dressing ingredients into the jar and give it a shake, let settle, then pile in the salad ingredients in layers, starting with the chickpeas and ending with the salad leaves.
2. Pop the lid on and bring to school or work, give it all a good shake and eat from the jar or tip into a bowl. You can add a fresh avocado, but only at the last minute.
3. Wide-mouthed jars are best. I find empty chocolate-spread ones great – and free!

Cantonese Cucumber Salad

A fresh and zingy salad, just bursting with fresh flavours, perfect to serve with the duck spring rolls on page 78.

Serves 4 as a side salad
Ingredients
1 cucumber
4 tbsp light soy sauce
2 tbsp Chinese vinegar
2 tbsp sesame oil
1 fresh chilli, any type, finely chopped and deseeded

Method

1. Wash the cucumber and wrap it tightly in a tea-towel or cloth and, with the back of a heavy knife or cleaver, smash it up. The cucumber will fall naturally into long chunks when pulled apart; this allows all the flavours of the marinade to infuse.
2. Mix the remaining ingredients and leave the cucumber to soak in the dressing for at least 2 hours before serving.

Spicy South-East Asian Veggie Salad

Like an Asian slaw but much more more-ish, this is a winner with grilled fish or roast chicken thighs and is strangely addictive. Shredding all the vegetables makes it more appealing to kids too. Sprouting pulses and seeds makes them more digestible and far more nutritious, so be sure to have some handy, but you can buy bean sprouts too.

Serves 4 as a side dish

Ingredients

200g mung bean sprouts

50g mixed sprouts

1 carrot, shredded by peeling it with a potato peeler

2 peppers, mixed colours, cut into thin strips

10g mushrooms, cut into thin slices

Dressing

2 cloves garlic, crushed

1 thumb-sized piece of ginger, grated

½ fresh red chilli, chopped finely and deseeded

4 tbsp soy sauce

2 tbsp fresh lime juice

4 tbsp light olive oil

1 tbsp honey

Fresh coriander, basil and mint – a big handful of each, rolled up and chopped

Method

1. Mix all the shredded and sliced veg together in a big bowl.
2. Mix all the dressing ingredients together, except for the herbs, and toss this onto the veg, giving everything a good stir. Add in the herbs and toss again. Leave to marinade for an hour at least so that all the veg can wilt a little and the flavours mingle. Taste for seasoning and enjoy!
3. You can add some leftover shredded chicken and rice noodles to this for a main course lunch.

Sprouting Seeds

Sprouting seeds, grains and legumes is easy and makes them not only more digestible, but also increases their B vitamins and vitamin C. Adding a few sprouts to salads, soups, stews or sandwiches is an easy way to load up on these nutrients. A small amount is enough, however, a teaspoon to a tablespoon a day will give you all the extra vitamins you need.

Different seeds and grains, like buckwheat, kidney beans, chickpeas, mung beans, sunflower seeds and almonds take different times to germinate, but the process couldn't be easier.

Get a jar with a lid and make a loose 'cover' with a piece of muslin and an elastic band. Take a tablespoon of seeds or pulses and soak them overnight. Rinse them and drain away the water through the mesh 'lid'. Leave the jar upside down on your draining board or on a wire rack that's on top of a tea towel. You can also buy special sprouting kits. The seeds or grains should be rinsed and drained twice a day until their sprout appears.

Don't be alarmed if a bloom appears overnight, this will rinse away. Once the sprouts are ready, replace the loose cover with the proper lid of the jar and store them in the fridge for a few days as you use them. Repeat the process to ensure you always have a stash of these little superfoods.

Stocks and Soups

Basic Chicken Stock

I remember clearly perching on a chair beside the cooker, as a young girl, while my mum put the bones from a roast chicken into a pot, covered it with water and added a peeled onion, carrot and a small bunch of herbs. We used to have this clear chicken soup before a meal of my favourite chicken casserole (page 70). Making this chicken stock, or broth, has been an integral part of my cooking in the past number of years. It's quite simple really, and the taste and health benefits make it worth the effort.

For making stocks and soups, it really is worth investing in a good, heavy-bottomed pot, ideally 10-litre as, once the ingredients are in, you need enough space for lots of water and vegetables. I've recently converted to using a slow cooker, a cheap and fantastic kitchen tool. Making stock in this overnight means that none of it will evaporate and you get the best flavours. To make stock you can use a whole raw chicken, the bones from your roast dinner, or a raw chicken carcass. If you use a good-quality chicken, you will get good quality stock. It's difficult these days to get giblets with a chicken, but if you can then add these to the pot too. The feet also add valuable flavour and gelatin.

You can easily swap some of your daily mugs of tea for a mug of this once you get into a habit of making it; it soothes your body and your soul, one version is known as 'Jewish penicillin' – it's basically a hug in a mug!

Makes as much as your pot will take

Ingredients
Bones/carcass from one chicken, either raw or cooked. (Roasted bones will add great flavour)
Chicken giblets, neck, feet, if you can get them
2 onions, peeled and cut into quarters
2 sticks celery, washed and cut into chunks
2 carrots, peeled and cut into chunks
2 cloves garlic, peeled and left whole
6 whole peppercorns
2 bay leaves
1 tsp sea salt

Method
1. Put all the ingredients into a large pot, and fill the pot with enough cold water to cover everything. Put the pot on to boil; keep an eye on it as scum will appear on the surface. Skim this off with a slotted spoon and discard it.
2. Once the pot is boiling, turn the heat down and allow it to simmer gently for 4-10 hours, or cook on medium in your slow cooker overnight. This seems like a very long time, but the slow cooking results in a flavoursome stock that has all the goodness drawn out from the bones.
3. Once the stock is cooked, ladle some into a mug and top with freshly chopped parsley and a sprinkle of sea salt, if needed. Enjoy the warming goodness.
4. Leave the stock to go cold and strain it, discarding the cooked bones and veg. You can now freeze the stock in clean glass jars or plastic tubs for later use. The strained stock will keep for about 4 days covered in the fridge. Use this as a base for any soups you make.

Pho Ga Vietnamese Noodle Soup

If you travel to Vietnam you will no doubt eat vast quantities of this delicious and vibrant noodle soup. A great meal in itself that ticks many boxes, *pho* (pronounced 'fuh') is a soup that's all about the stock pot and each *pho* cook has his or her own closely-guarded secrets. Vietnamese eat this mostly for breakfast, topping their soup with a squeeze of lime, a pile of fresh herbs and a few chillies. Noodle soup of many origins is widely available in Asian restaurants, from *ramen* to *pho*.

For an authentic Asian experience, be sure to get lots of fresh herbs, mint, purple basil and coriander. Once you have your chicken stock, fresh or frozen, yours is a blank canvas onto which you can paint all your flavours. You will need large bowls for serving this.

Serves 4
Ingredients
1½ litres chicken stock
Fish sauce, for sprinkling
1 stick lemongrass, bashed with the side of a knife
Rice noodles, to serve 4
2-4 raw or cooked chicken breasts
Large bunches fresh mint, purple or regular basil, coriander
Lime wedges, 4
Sliced red chillies, optional

Method
1. Heat up the stock and add the lemongrass. If you're using raw chicken, slice the breasts and slide them into the stock. Simmer for at least five minutes, until cooked with no traces of pink remaining.
2. Meanwhile cook the noodles according to the packet instructions and divide between the bowls.
3. Place the cooked chicken on top of the noodles, pour over the hot chicken stock, sprinkle each bowl lightly with fish sauce and top liberally with the fresh herbs – or just put the herbs on a plate on the table for people to help themselves
4. Serve with a plate of lime wedges – a squeeze of lime really finishes off the dish – and add a few sliced red chillies to your bowl if you dare!

Variation
For a change from noodles, you could replace them with spiralised vegetables.

Beef Bone Broth 🍜

Eating bone marrow – that white, spongey substance from inside bones – is said to aid digestive health and improve immunity. It's also delicious and is served as a delicacy in many restaurants, often roasted with sea salt and served alongside a juicy steak. Ask your butcher for some beef bones, cut into pieces about 5cm deep, shin bones are good for this recipe. Place them on a roasting tray, sprinkle lightly with sea-salt and roast for 1½ hours until the marrow bubbles up. You can eat the marrow straight away; simply scoop it out and enjoy.

This stock is based on a French style of cooking; the sweating of the vegetables will result in a rich and flavoursome broth. If you don't want to bother with this step then simply put everything in the pot and follow the steps for making chicken stock (p56).

Makes about 6-7 litres
Ingredients
6-8 beef bones
1-2 tbsp lard
2 large onions, peeled and cut into quarters
2 carrots peeled and cut into chunks
2 sticks celery, halved
4 whole cloves garlic, peeled
2 bay leaves
1 sprig thyme
12 peppercorns
2 tsp sea salt
1 tbsp white wine vinegar
Preheat the oven to 180C/350F/Gas Mark 4

Method

1. Roast the beef bones by sprinkling them with a little sea salt and roasting them on a large tray in the hot oven for an hour. Enjoy the roasted marrow; you can fish it out with a pointed knife before you add it to the stock pot.
2. Add the veg and herbs to the roasting dish, drizzle them with a little melted coconut oil or lard and return the tray to the oven for 30 minutes for the veg to take on some colour.
3. Tip everything into your stock pot and deglaze the roasting tray by pouring on some hot water and scraping off any 'goodness' into the pot. Top up with cold water to reach below the top of the pot. You can follow these steps if you want to make your stock in a slow cooker too.
4. Bring the pot to a boil, skimming off any scum as it boils, reduce the heat to a very gentle simmer and allow it to cook for 4-10 hours, or overnight on medium in your slow cooker.
5. Strain the stock and discard the bones and veg. Use the broth as a warming beef tea or as a base for other soups and stews.

Some Warming Soups

Chunky Chickpea and Chorizo Soup

Chickpeas, tins of tomatoes and chorizo are useful to have in your store cupboard. Add in some orzo pasta or brown rice and you'll never be without a quick meal. This is a handy winter warmer and perfect to bring to school, college or work to keep you going during the day.

Serves 2-4

Ingredients

1 tbsp olive oil
1 onion, chopped
1 clove garlic peeled and chopped
100g chorizo, roughly chopped
½ tsp cayenne pepper
400g tin chickpeas, drained and rinsed
400g tin chopped tomatoes
500ml stock, chicken or vegetable
Handful orzo or similar small pasta
Fresh parsley or coriander to serve

Method

1. Heat some olive oil and cook the onion and garlic with the chorizo for 5 minutes, then add the cayenne pepper, tomatoes and stock and bring to a bubble and cook for 10 minutes.
2. Add in the chickpeas and orzo if using, continue to cook for another 10 minutes.
3. Season and serve with plenty of chopped herbs.

Nettle Soup

Nettles are known to be high in iron. Only pick the tops and ideally far from a busy road. If you grab the nettles hard they won't sting you, but if in doubt, wear gloves. The sting goes out of them as soon as they are cooked.

Serves 4-6

Ingredients

250g freshly picked nettles, washed with big stems cut off
1 onion, chopped
30g butter
2 medium-sized potatoes, peeled and diced
1½ litres stock, chicken or vegetable
Nutmeg
Sea salt and black pepper
Wild garlic flowers, to garnish

Method

1. In a large, heavy-bottomed pot melt the butter and cook the onion with the potato slowly for about 10 minutes.
2. Add in the nettles and give them a good stir to wilt, pour on the stock.
3. Bring everything to a bubble and turn down the heat and allow to cook for 15 minutes. Give it a blitz in the blender or with a stick blender.
4. Season to taste and add a little grated nutmeg.
5. Serve decorated with a few fresh wild garlic flowers, which are out when the nettles first appear in spring.

Spicy Sweet Potato and Coconut Soup

Sweet potato is a tasty and easy way to get good carbs into you at a low cost. It's great for pancakes and bakes, but especially good for soups as it cooks fast. I like to add a bit of spice to balance out the sweetness. Butternut squash works equally well.

Serves 2-4
Ingredients
1 onion, chopped
2 tbsp coconut or olive oil
2 cloves garlic peeled and chopped
600g sweet potato/1 large sweet potato, peeled and chopped roughly into chunks
½ tsp cayenne pepper
500ml stock, chicken or veg
½ 400ml can coconut milk, or you can add the full can if you don't find it too rich
Salt, pepper and coriander, to serve

Method

1. In a large pot, heat the oil and cook the onion and garlic for 5 minutes until soft.
2. Add the sweet potatoes and cayenne and stir, allow to cook for a minute or so.
3. Pour in the stock and add the coconut milk, stir to combine everything and let it bubble for 10 minutes.
4. Zap everything in the blender and it's ready. Season with a little sea salt and pepper and serve, drizzled with a little coconut milk and sprinkled with fresh coriander.

Minestrone

Using brown rice instead of pasta makes this meal in a bowl into a gluten-free feast. Using a flavour-loaded, deep-green kale like *cavalo nero* will give you a delicious soup where you can taste all the different ingredients in each spoonful. Top with shaved Parmesan and serve with a hunk of crusty bread and you have the perfect winter warmer that's also really good for you.

Serves 4-6

Ingredients

1 onion, chopped
2 cloves garlic, finely chopped
2 carrots, peeled and diced
2 sticks celery, diced
2-4 tbsp olive oil
50ml white wine, optional
100g brown basmati rice, preferably soaked for at least an hour
400g tin cannellini beans
2 large tomatoes
2 litres fresh chicken stock or vegetable stock, heated up for the soup
2 large handfuls kale, washed and roughly chopped
Sea salt and pepper
Parmesan cheese for serving

Method

1. In a large, heavy-bottomed pot, heat the oil over a medium heat and gently fry the onion, garlic, carrot and celery. Put a lid on the pot and allow the veg to 'sweat' for about 15 minutes.
2. Strain the rice through a sieve and rinse it, turn up the heat and add it to the pot. Give it a good stir and add the wine, if using. This will give the soup a deep, intense flavour. Let it bubble for a few minutes to burn off the alcohol.
3. Add the stock to the pot with the tomatoes. Cook for 20 minutes on a simmer. Check to see if the rice is nearly done and then add the beans and the kale and cook gently for a further 10 minutes.
4. Taste the soup and season with sea salt and black pepper. Ladle into bowls and top with Parmesan shavings. The gentle cooking of this soup ensures you still have all the different colours and textures in your bowl.
5. Enjoy with a glass of that white wine you opened!

Winning Dinners

My Mum's Chicken Casserole

Growing up this was one of my favourite dinners, and still is. It takes a bit of time to make, but can be prepared ahead of time then enjoyed later in the day. This recipe uses every part of the chicken – you make the stock from the carcass, which gives a huge amount of flavour.

Ingredients

1 medium chicken, skinned and jointed
1 leek
100g flour
2 tomatoes
100g field or regular white mushrooms
2 tbsp olive oil and 50ml butter, for frying
Salt and pepper
Preheat oven 180C/350F/Gas 5

Method

1. Skin and joint the chicken into 8 pieces. Make the stock by bringing the carcass to the boil in a pot with a washed chopped leek and enough water to cover it all, and simmering for an hour.

2. Put the flour onto a plate and mix in some salt and pepper to season it, or put it into a Ziploc bag. You want to coat your chicken pieces in the flour so either press them onto the flour on both sides and dust off the excess, or pop them into the bag, a few at a time, and shake it to coat them.

3. Heat the butter and oil in a wide, deep frying pan. Brown the pieces of floured chicken all over and remove, placing the browned pieces into a separate casserole pot (one that you have a lid for) as you continue with the others. Don't crowd the frying pan as the temperature will drop too much and they won't seal properly.

4. When all the chicken is browned, pour the remaining flour from your plate or bag into the pan. Stir the flour around lots to cook it and press it into all the juicy bits of the pan until you have some nice dark brown 'breadcrumbs'. This should take about 8 minutes.

5. Have your hot stock at the ready and ladle some of it into the pan, it will thicken the flour so start stirring. As you add more stock and keep stirring, it will turn into a nice, silky sauce after a few minutes. You want a thick soup texture. Let the sauce cook for 3-5 minutes on a low bubble. Season with a little sea salt and black pepper.

6. Pour the sauce over the browned chicken in the casserole; don't worry if it doesn't cover the meat as the added veg will release plenty of liquid in the cooking.

7. Slice the tomatoes and mushrooms and pop them into the casserole on top of the chicken.

8. Put a tight-fitting lid on the pot and cook it in the oven for an hour, then give it a gentle stir. If the sauce seems a bit thick, simply add a little hot stock to loosen it up. Serve with lots of fluffy mashed potatoes.

Cuban Chicken Rice

I've only been to Cuba once, but have been aching to get back there since. A country full of contradictions and music, teeming with life and energy, Cuba gets under your skin in more ways than one. The country now has an impressive system of 'organipónicos' or urban organic farms where communities grow and share fruit and veggies. This is a recipe for their most popular Sunday meal; I've cooked it many times at home and really find it makes the most of simple ingredients.

Ingredients
Serves 4

1 medium free-range chicken jointed into 8 pieces
50g plain flour
1 tsp sweet or smoked paprika
50-100ml olive oil, for frying
1 onion, chopped
2 cloves garlic, chopped

400g rice, I use jasmine, but any good white or brown rice will work
500-700ml chicken stock
50ml tomato purée
400g tin kidney or black eyed beans
1 yellow pepper, chopped
Salt and pepper, to season
1 lemon cut into wedges, to serve
Handful of chopped coriander, to serve

Method

1. Get a ziplock bag, put the flour into it, add the paprika, salt and pepper and give it a shake. Now pop the chicken pieces into the bag a few at a time and give the bag a good shake to coat them. Shake off any excess flour.

2. Heat the oil in a large casserole that has a tight fitting lid and brown the chicken pieces, remove them from the pot and keep on a plate until they are all browned.

3. Heat a little more oil if needed and fry the onion and garlic until they are softened (about 5-7 minutes), add the uncooked rice to the pan and give it a good stir. Mix in the peppers and the drained and rinsed beans, season with a little salt and pepper.

4. Flatten down the rice and lay the chicken pieces neatly on top.

5. Mix the hot stock with the tomato purée in a jug and pour this over the whole dish, ensuring that the rice is fully covered with liquid, then bring it to a bubble.

6. Pop on a lid and reduce the heat to low and cook on top of the cooker for 40 minutes. The steam in the pot will ensure everything is properly cooked and the chicken stays lovely and moist.

7. Serve with lemon wedges and coriander, plenty of Cuban salsa music playing in the background, and maybe a mojito!

Hainan Chicken Rice

This recipe is based on the famous Hainan Chicken Rice I enjoyed many moons ago on a trip to Penang in Malaysia where there is an entire street devoted to chicken rice restaurants. Chicken rice is the simplest, yet most satisfying meal; clean and uncomplicated, yet totally nourishing. Traditionally, it's served as a portion of the cooked chicken alongside a bowl of the hot stock and jasmine rice that has been cooked in the chicken stock. Kids love this because of the different parts and because you get to add soy sauce!

Ingredients
Serves: 4-6

1 free range / organic chicken, whole
6 cloves
2 onions, peeled
3/4 cloves garlic, peeled
1 thumb-sized piece of ginger, peeled and sliced

2 star anise
12 peppercorns
1 tsp salt
1 piece kombu seaweed, optional
100g jasmine rice per person
Soy sauce, chopped red chilli, spring onions, chopped and coriander, chopped, to serve

Method

1. Pop the whole chicken into the pot and cover with cold water, stick the cloves into one of the peeled onions and add this to the pot along with the all the remaining onion, the garlic, star anise, peppercorns, salt and kombu (if using).

2. Put the pot onto the heat and slowly bring it to a boil (this will take a while). Take care to skim off any scum as this will affect the final stock. Skim it at least four times.

3. Once the pot is boiling turn the heat down to a tiny simmer, you just want the pot to bubble very gently.

4. Leave it to cook like this for an hour, then take the chicken out of the liquid using a large slotted spoon and strain it in a colander. The residual heat will continue cooking the chicken and will leave you with tender meat as well as a lovely clear chicken broth.

5. To cook the rice Hainan style, melt a little chicken skin in a medium pot until the fat begins to come out, add 100g rice per person to the pot and give it a stir. Pour over some of your hot chicken stock – enough to cover the rice by an extra 1cm of depth – clamp a tight lid on, turn the heat down to minimum and cook the rice for 20 minutes. When you take the lid off, fork the rice over to fluff it up.

6. You can cook it like this an hour or two before you need it, then serve your Hainan Rice with the chicken, the hot broth and perhaps some little dipping bowls of chilli sauce and soy sauce, or make a dipping sauce by stir-frying some ginger and garlic in sesame oil and mixing in some oyster sauce.

Take One Duck ... 🦆

In the supermarket poultry section you'll see a huge number of chickens to every whole duck. But duck isn't expensive and it also comes with that wonderful bag of giblets; heart, livers and neck. I was inspired by Tom Flavin to chef it up a bit and make several delicious things from just one bird.

First take your duck and portion it as you would a chicken, separating the leg and thigh portions and carefully slicing off the breasts. This will leave you with four clean portions – dinner for two for two days! If you are in the habit of roasting ducks you will have a store of duck fat in the fridge that you might use for roasting potatoes. As this recipe calls for duck fat, you might consider roasting one for dinner and keeping the fat in the fridge to use here in the confit recipe. Or see 'The Best Bits' (page 79) for duck fat tips.

Duck Confit

Duck confit is a huge seller in restaurants, but it's so easy to make at home. It will keep for weeks in the fridge if stored in the fat and all you have to do is reheat it in a hot oven for 10 minutes to bring it back to life. As a duck has two legs, all these recipes serve 2. You will need to salt the duck legs the night before you want to make this. Sprinkle a teaspoon of salt onto the legs, rub it in and cover them and leave them in the fridge.

Ingredients
500-1000ml duck fat melted in a heavy casserole, or tin with a lid
2 salted duck leg and thigh portions
You could add in the wings and the neck too, as the meat from
them can be used to make the spring rolls
Oven 150C/320F/Gas4

Method
1. Pop the duck portions into the fat and bring it to a bubble on the hob, now put the lid on the casserole and pop it into the oven for 2-3 hours. When the duck is cooked you can leave it in the fat, in a container in the fridge or you can eat it straight away by removing it from the fat and popping it under the grill for five minutes to crisp it up. You can store your duck confit with the duck meat fully submerged in its fat in a large, sterilised jar in the fridge for several weeks.
2. To eat the duck, remove it from the fat and pop it on a roasting tray and reheat it at 200C/400F/Gas6 for 15-20 minutes for a lovely roasted, full-flavoured ducky treat.
3. I love duck with cabbage, either sauerkraut (page 137-8), braised red cabbage or green cabbage lightly sautéed with some bacon bits or some ginger.

Pan-fried Duck Breasts

Duck has so much of its own fat which is rendered in the pan as it cooks so you don't need to add any oil to the pan.

Ingredients

2 duck breasts
Salt and pepper

Method

1. Score the breasts in a criss-cross pattern with a sharp knife, season the skin with a little sea salt and black pepper. Heat up a cast-iron or heavy frying pan; the pan should be very hot to start cooking.

2. Place the breast skin-side down on the pan to sizzle, now turn the heat down to medium and watch as all the fat renders away from under the skin. After about 10 minutes turn the breasts over and cook for 3-4 minutes on the other side if you want the meat medium rare, or cook for longer if you prefer it more well done. Remove the breasts from the pan onto a plate and leave to rest in a warm oven for at least 5 minutes.

3. Slice the breasts neatly into thin slices and arrange on warm plates, serve with some warmed sauerkraut made with red cabbage, page 137-8 or with some hoisin sauce that you can buy from Asian supermarkets.

Duck Spring Rolls

Using the meat from the neck and wings you can easily make delicious spring rolls. Simply stir fry some ginger in a wok with some carrots cut finely into sticks, cook this for about five minutes and add some bean sprouts and the duck meat, sprinkle over a dash of soy sauce and cook for a further minute. Throw in some chopped fresh coriander and sliced spring onions. Spring roll wrappers can be bought from any Asian supermarket. Spread one out on a work surface and spoon on some filling near a corner facing you, wet the edges and fold over the corner, then fold in the sides and roll the whole thing up tightly. Use up all your filling to make more rolls and heat up some oil in a wide pan. Shallow fry your spring rolls until they are golden and lift them out to drain. Cut at an angle and serve with hoisin sauce for dipping.

Pan Fried Duck Livers and Hearts

I've been enjoying duck livers fried in butter as a snack or as part of a salad for years; the heart is tasty too, just slice it in half and remove any tough ventricles. Simply melt some butter on a pan and when it's bubbling pop the livers and heart into it. Leave them cook for about a minute and turn them over and cook for a further minute, spoon on to a plate and drizzle over the pan juices. These are great on a nice piece of toasted sourdough as a quick lunch or even breakfast.

The Best Bits

So, after making the recipes above, you have a duck car-cass and lots of excess fat, you can put all of these onto a roasting tray, spreading out the duck skin and sprinkle it all with some sea salt. Put it in the oven and roast it for about 1-1 1/2 hours until all the fat has melted and the skin is crispy. Pour the fat into jars (this can be used for duck confit) and refrigerate for further cooking and chow down on the delicious crispy, ducky snacks. The roasted carcass can be used for extra meat pickings for spring rolls or a salad and then boiled to make stock.

Braised Shin Beef with Bone Marrow and Vegetables

My mum used to make a great version of this. Once it was cooked, she would blitz the roast vegetables to make a sauce that was full of flavour. My lads won't eat a vegetably sauce like that, so we have the juices and I have the chunks of tender veg; either way is yummy. I use shin beef as it has the bone marrow (which is just too good to waste) intact.

Ingredients
Serves 4

4 pieces of shin beef with the marrow in
1/4 turnip peeled and cut into chunks
2-3 large carrots, peeled and cut into large chunks
2 medium onions, peeled and cut into large chunks
100ml olive oil or lard, for frying
200ml beef stock as per p60 or 200ml water flavoured with 2tbsp Worcestershire sauce
Sea salt and pepper
Preheat oven 180C/350F/Gas4

Method

1. In a heavy-bottomed casserole heat the oil or lard and brown the meat on both sides; you'll need to brown the meat in batches to avoid crowding the pan.
2. Remove the meat to a plate, throw the veggies onto the pan and brown them, stirring them around to get a bit of colour.
3. Lay the meat on top of the veggies in casserole.
4. Season the stock or water with salt and pepper, give it a stir and pour this into the casserole from the side, the water should only just cover the veg, put a lid on it and fire it into the oven.
5. After 20 minutes turn the heat down to 150C/320F/Gas3 and leave it to cook for a further 2 1/2 hours. Turn off the oven a half an hour before you want to eat the meat and leave it in the cooling oven.
6. Serve the meat over mashed potatoes and spoon over the juices and veg.
7. You can do a similar thing with a shoulder of lamb, not rolled or boned. Just brown it in the same way and lay it on the veg, be sure to add some rosemary and garlic to the mix and cook it under foil in the same way as you will need to use a big roasting tin. The lamb will be deliciously tender with nice browned bits on the outside.

BRAISED SHIN BEEF WITH BONE MARROW AND VEGETABLES 81

Whole Roasted Sea Bream with Olives and Lemons

Every time I cook fish I say to myself that I really should cook it more. It's so easy to do something delicious with it and never fails to be yummy. I first tasted this dish when I ate it in the Cornstore Restaurant in Limerick, cooked by the amazing chef Maura Baxter. The whole fish looks great and the addition of olives, cherry tomatoes and lemon made it one of the nicest things I've ever eaten. Make sure the fish have bright clear eyes when you buy them. This is a very Greek dish – one of my favourite countries to visit.

Serves a hungry pair or 4 medium appetites

Ingredients

2 medium to large sea bream
2 large vines of cherry tomatoes
2 handfuls stoned kalamata olives
2 lemons, cut into wedges
Olive oil
Sea salt and pepper
Preheat the oven to 200C/F375/Gas5

Method

1. Ask the fishmonger to scale and clean the fish and cut off the pointy fins. Ideally, leave the heads on. Slash shallow cuts into both sides of the fish.
2. Take a large roasting tray and lay the tomato vines into the tray.
3. Stone the olives by laying them on a board and crushing them with the side of a large knife; the stone should just slide out.
4. Scatter the olives around the tomatoes, add the lemon wedges to the dish, lay the fish on top and drizzle olive oil over everything, finish with a good sprinkling of salt and pepper.
5. Roast in the oven for 25 minutes until the fish skin gets nice and crispy, serve with baby new potato salad p114 and a green salad.

Bacon and Cabbage Risotto

Why not? The flavours work so well with potatoes, why not in this creamy, delicious and indulgent dish? People often shy away from making risotto as you do have to stand by the pot and stir it regularly, but you will have a meal ready in 30 minutes or less so it's really not that big a deal. Whenever I have left-over chicken stock, I make risotto; it's handy to keep a couple of those small bottles of wine in the cupboard as the wine really makes a difference to the end result. Risotto is versatile, so try a blue cheese and chorizo combo or the classic pea and prawn.

Makes 2 servings

Ingredients

50ml olive oil

1 small onion, finely chopped

1 stick celery, washed and finely chopped

1 litre chicken or vegetable stock

200g risotto rice

150ml white wine

200g bacon bits or lardons

2-4 large cabbage leaves, washed with the spines taken out and shredded

Salt and pepper

100g butter

100g Parmesan cheese

Method

1. Heat the oil in a heavy-bottomed pan and gently fry the onion and celery for about 5-7 minutes until they soften.

2. Meanwhile put the stock in a pot to heat it up; have a ladle handy.

3. Add the rice to the pot and give it a good stir to coat it.

4. Now add the wine and stir it well, turn up the heat so that the wine evaporates.

5. Add the bacon bits to the pan with the cabbage and stir everything to coat.

6. Ladle in some stock, add a pinch of salt and a shake or two of black pepper to the pot and stir well.

7. Stir the pot every minute or so to ensure the rice doesn't stick to the bottom.

8. Add more stock and salt and pepper, repeating the process until the rice stops absorbing and is looking creamy and has a slight bite to it.

9. Now turn off the heat and add your butter and Parmesan cheese to the pot, don't stir it, just cover it and leave it for a few minutes for everything to melt. Now stir it and your risotto is ready! Enjoy this Irish twist on an Italian classic!

Pork and Bean Chowder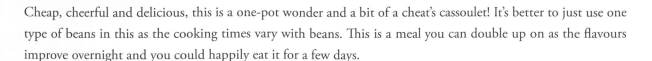

Cheap, cheerful and delicious, this is a one-pot wonder and a bit of a cheat's cassoulet! It's better to just use one type of beans in this as the cooking times vary with beans. This is a meal you can double up on as the flavours improve overnight and you could happily eat it for a few days.

Serves 4
Ingredients
200g dried white haricot beans, soaked overnight
1 onion, chopped
2 cloves garlic, crushed
4 tbsp olive oil
500g piece pork belly cut into chunks about 2cm thick
200ml cider (optional)
2 x 400g tins tomatoes/ 1 1/2 bottles passata (What size bottle / tins?)
1 sprig thyme
Grated cheddar, to serve
Salt and pepper

Method
1. Cook the dried beans for 20 minutes in a pressure cooker (release the pressure slowly so that the skins don't separate), or you can simply boil the beans hard for 10 minutes then turn the heat down and simmer them on a medium heat for about an hour until they are tender, but not mush. Drain and reserve the cooking liquid, which you may need later.
2. In a large pot, heat the oil and gently fry the onion and garlic for about 10 minutes until soft. Add the meat and cook on all sides until well-browned. If you feel there is too much fat in the pan at this stage then tip out some into a jar.
3. Add the cider, if using, and boil for a couple of minutes for the alcohol (but not the flavour) to cook off, add the tomatoes, herbs and half a can of water to the pot, then add in the beans. Bring everything to a bubble and then reduce the heat and cook for about 40 minutes; if it starts to look a bit dry, just add some of the bean-cooking liquid.
4. Serve in large bowls, sprinkled with cheddar cheese and a decent loaf of crusty bread to mop up the lovely tomatoey juices.

Veggie Variation

If you don't eat meat you can still pack lots of flavour into this dish by using 500g of diced carrots, courgette and celery instead of the meat; remember that good, home-grown or organic veggies will give you much more flavour. You could also try using black eyed or kidney beans in place of haricot and add some cayenne pepper and cumin.

Baked Butternut Squash Stuffed with Cheese

Don't be fooled by the slouchy appearance of this dish, the big flavours and richness of the ingredients will leave you more than satisfied. This makes an excellent vegetarian main course or goes really well alongside a Sunday roast chicken.

Serves 2 as a main course, 4 as a side dish
Ingredients
1 medium butternut squash
1 carton crème fraiche
100g grated Parmesan cheese
1 tsp cumin seeds
Drizzle of olive oil, for baking
1 tbsp fresh sage leaves, finely chopped
Sea salt and black pepper
Preheat the oven to 180C/350F/Gas 4

Method
1. Cut the squash in half lengthways – don't peel it – scoop out the seeds and score the flesh with a knife in a criss-cross pattern, this helps it cook through faster. Place it on a baking tray and drizzle over a little olive oil, rubbing it in, and sprinkle over the cumin seeds. Bake in a hot oven for 30-40 minutes until it is soft enough for a knife to go through it easily.
2. Remove it from the oven and, with a dessert spoon, carefully scoop out most of the flesh into a large bowl, taking care not to cut the skin; you want the shell to remain intact.
3. Add the créme fraiche, the grated cheese, chopped sage, some sea salt and ground black pepper, mix this all together and spoon it back into the cases. Sprinkle on some extra cheese.
4. Return the squash to the oven and bake for a further 20-30 minutes until golden brown and bubbling – the more browned, crispy bits the better.

Prawns Two Ways

Prawns are so easy and fast to cook, a sweet and juicy treat and perfect for when you want to spoil yourself.

Simple Pan-Fried Prawns

Serves 1

Ingredients

Prawns, as many as you like, I take off the head and peel them, leaving the tail on, as it looks nice
50ml olive oil
1 garlic clove, chopped
Juice of 1/2 a lemon
Parsley, chopped, to garnish
Sea salt and pepper

Method

1. Heat the oil in the pan and lay on the prawns one by one. As soon as you have laid the last prawn, turn over the first – that's how fast they cook! Add the garlic, squeeze over the juice of half a lemon, sprinkle on some salt and pepper and a small handful of chopped parsley. You can have this with some crusty bread or add it to a bowl of spaghetti, be sure to have a glass of white wine too!

Chraimeh Prawns

This chraimeh dish is something I tasted in a roadside restaurant when I went to visit my brother who was living in Bahrain at the time. We went to lots of very swanky restaurants, but the food in this little, plastic-furnished place was the best I've tasted in that part of the world. It's worth making up a batch of this spice mix so you have an instant treat when you want; once you have the spice made, the dish is ready to serve in minutes.

Ingredients

300g fresh raw prawns, peeled
4 tbsp light olive oil
6 cloves garlic, chopped
2 tsp paprika
1 tbsp caraway seeds
1 tsp cumin seeds
1/2 tsp cayenne pepper
1/4 tsp ground cinnamon

1 green chilli, chopped
150ml water
3 tbsp tomato purée
2 tsp sugar
2 tbsp lemon juice
Salt and pepper
Chopped coriander, to serve
Lemon wedges, to serve

Method

1. Dry toast the caraway and cumin on a frying pan, grind them in the mortar and pestle, then add the remaining spices and the garlic and chilli, stir in 2 tbsp light olive oil and keep grinding until it has a nice pasty texture.

2. Heat 2 tbsp oil in a heavy frying pan and fry the prawns as in the recipe above. Remove them from the pan and set aside.

3. Throw the spice paste into the pan and give it a good stir, cooking it for at least one minute, add the water and tomato purée and stir, then add the lemon juice and sugar.

4. Season to taste, then lay the prawns back in the pan and let them heat through for a minute.

5. Serve this with some fresh coriander, lemon wedges and some warmed pitas or plain boiled rice. Too tasty for words.

Thai Coconut Milk Curry

The very first time I tasted a Thai curry was in Thailand – no surprise there! As I marvelled at the spices and flavours and wondered what lengthy process would be needed to make such an invigorating and lively sauce the chef hurried off and came back with a packet, showing it enthusiastically to me. It was a yellow curry paste, with all the hard work done. If it's authentic enough for Thailand, it's good enough for me. Using pumpkin or squash works well in this dish as the chunks soak up all the delicious flavours and don't fall apart. The best varieties to use are Ichi Kuri or butternut squash. This curry is equally good with chicken, vegetables or prawns. As Thai curries are more liquid than Indian ones they can seem like soups; you can adjust the stock for the consistency you prefer. You can make this with butternut squash at any time of year, but in autumn you can find cute squash like baby bear, cut them open, spoon out the inside and serve the curry inside, like in the photograph.

Serves 2-4
Ingredients
1/2 a butternut or Ichi Kuri squash, peeled and cut into chunks of 3cm square(ish)

400g can coconut milk

2 tbsp oil, vegetable of sunflower

2tbsp Thai yellow curry paste, available from all Asian food shops

200g cooked chicken or 2 chicken breasts, raw and sliced or 200g prawns, fresh or frozen

60g frozen petit pois or regular frozen peas, allowed to defrost

500ml chicken or vegetable stock

1 lime, cut into wedges

2 tbsp Thai fish sauce

Handful coriander and mint, to serve

Method
1. Heat the oil in a medium pan and fry the curry paste for 2 minutes, add the coconut milk and the stock and bring to a simmer.

2. Add the chunks of pumpkin or squash and allow them to cook for 15-20 minutes, then add your chicken or prawns. Simmer everything for a further 5 minutes, do not let it boil or the curry will split.

3. To serve, ladle the soup into bowls add some fish sauce, squeeze over some lime juice and sprinkle with fresh coriander and mint.

4. Serve this curry with some steamed Thai jasmine rice.

Baked Treats

Breakfast Bagels

Often when you buy bagels, what you're getting is a dry bread roll with a hole in the middle; real bagels are poached, then baked, this is what gives them their fantastic, glossy, chewy crust. These slightly 'healthier' bagels use granary flour and lots of seeds for added flavour and textures, but you can make plain white bagels by using only strong white flour in this recipe in the place of brown.

Makes about 16
Ingredients
1kg strong brown bread flour or granary flour
60g mixed sunflower and pumpkin seeds, preferably soaked for an hour
2 tbsp sugar
3tsp sea salt
3tsp fresh or 1.5tsp fast action yeast
600ml tepid water
2 tbsp malt or sugar for boiling the bagels
4 tbsp extra mixed seeds, for sprinkling

Method
1. Put the flour, sugar and salt into a large bowl or the mixing bowl of an electric mixer, crumble in the fresh yeast or sprinkle in the fast-action, pour in the water and mix everything together until it is combined into a craggy ball.
2. Using the dough hook on your mixer, or by hand, knead the dough for 10 minutes until smooth and elastic.
3. Pop the dough in a bowl, cover with a tea-towel or a piece of oiled clingfilm and leave in a warm place to rise for an hour until doubled in size.
4. Punch the risen dough down in the bowl and tip it out onto a lightly floured surface. Portion the dough into 50g balls, or roll the dough out into two long sausages and cut it into 16 equal-ish portions. the easiest way to portion is to cut off a chunk of dough and weigh each piece, but it doesn't have to be too accurate.
5. Take each piece, roll it into a little ball and poke a hole in it with your finger; wiggle your finger round so the hole gets bigger. When all the bagels have their holes made, lay them on oiled baking sheets, covered with more oiled clingfilm, and leave to rise for 20 minutes.
6. Meanwhile preheat the oven to 220C/425F/ Gas 7 and bring a large pot of water to a boil. Add the sugar to the boiling water and pop the risen bagels in, a few at a time, boil for 1 minute, turning them once with a slotted spoon.
7. Remove the bagels from the water, place them back onto the oiled baking sheets, sprinkle with the remaining seeds and bake in the preheated oven for 10-15 minutes until golden brown and shiny. Enjoy every chewy morsel!

Best-Ever Brownies

There are many brownie recipes in the world, and many things that claim to be brownies but are just sad brown squares of powdery, dry cake. Brownies should deliver fudginess and happiness, and this one – based on one from the queen of cooking – Nigella – does just that. I baked these brownies for my children until my youngest son took over and now does them so well that my work is done! All I can say here is 'read the recipe' – use the mixer at the right stage, fold when it says fold, or you will end up with a brick. We always make these the day before we need them as they need time to set in the tin.

Ingredients

400g good quality dark chocolate, minimum 70% cocoa solids
400g butter
500g caster sugar
6 medium sized eggs
1 tsp vanilla extract
200g plain white or white spelt flour
Preheat the oven 170C/340F/Gas 4
Line a 30 x 40cm roasting tin at least 5cm deep with foil, push the foil in well to the sides

Method

1. Break up the chocolate by smashing the bars off the side of the worktop in their packets, when you open them it will be in bits and you can just pour it into a saucepan to melt it.
2. Chop the butter and add it to the chocolate and melt it over a low heat while stirring gently. Turn off the heat.
3. Meanwhile put the sugar, egg mixture and vanilla into a bowl and whisk on high speed until it's light and fluffy, this will take about 5 minutes.
4. Pour the chocolate mixture onto the eggs and stir slowly to combine fully – don't use the mixer after this stage.
5. Sieve the flour in one third at a time and fold it after each addition until the flour is fully incorporated.
6. When all the flour is added pour the mixture into the lined tin, getting it all out with a spatula and giving the bowl to a lucky baking helper, or licking it yourself. Tip the tin around so that the mixture is even. Bake in the centre of the oven for 20-22 minutes.
7. Take the tin out and leave it to cool fully before cutting, overnight is best.
8. The easiest way to cut these is to lift the whole lot out on the foil, lay it on a board and peel off the sides of the foil. Use a large chopping knife or cleaver slice the slab into 20 pieces and carefully lift them off the foil. Make new friends and influence people with these!

Chocolate Beetroot Brownies

These are sexy brownies, no other way to say it! They're moist, delicious, gluten-free – and so nutritious, it's better for you to eat them than not!

Ingredients

200g dark chocolate, min 70% cocoa solids
100g butter or coconut oil
1 tsp vanilla extract
2 medium-sized cooked beetroots (I cook beetroot by dry-roasting them for 2 hours. When they're cool, just peel the skin off with a knife) or you can use vacuum-packed ones from the shops, just make sure they have no vinegar in them
2 eggs
100ml pure maple syrup
150g ground almonds
Preheat oven 170degreesC/340F/Gas4
Line a small baking tin, about 20cm x 10cm with foil

Method

1. Break up the chocolate and put it in a thick-bottomed pot with the butter, heat gently until it's all melted together, stir gently while melting.
2. Add the vanilla and leave to cool slightly, slowly stir in the maple syrup.
3. Blitz the cooked beets in a blender and add to the mix.
4. Beat the eggs in one by one, sprinkle on the ground almonds and stir in until well combined.
5. Pour the mix into the prepared tin and bake for 25-30 minutes until slightly risen.
6. Take out of the oven and leave to set until almost completely cold, cut gently and devour with cream, ice cream or créme fraiche, and a few raspberries.

Coconut Bread

Every time my best buddy Linda comes home from the UK we go on a big night out; recently we started an epicurean game – one of us goes to the bar for cocktails and the other has to guess the subtle ingredients like elderflower or wasabi in the drink, not always as easy as it sounds! On one trip she tasted one that reminded her of a coconut bread she'd had in Sydney. I've never been to Oz and had never heard of coconut bread, but was intrigued so she sent me a recipe, which I altered dramatically, adding some gluten-free flour to lighten the mix to stop it becoming too dense. It's delicious and highly addictive and best with lots of butter.

Makes one loaf
Ingredients
100g coconut flour, available from Asian foodstores
100g dessicated coconut
150g gluten-free plain flour/ white spelt/ plain flour
1 tsp baking powder
250g/10oz coconut yogurt/ coconut milk/ coconut kefir
3 eggs
Grated zest 1 lime
60ml/4 tbsp maple syrup
Preheat oven to 170C/340F/Gas3
Prepare a 2lb loaf tin by rubbing the insides with oil or butter

Method
1. In a large bowl, mix the dry ingredients, including the lime zest, together keeping a little for serving.
2. In a jug or bowl, mix together the remaining ingredients.
3. Pour the wet ingredients into the dry and stir well with a large spoon to combine fully.
4. Spoon the batter into the prepared tin and bake in the centre of the preheated oven for 45 minutes – if a cocktail stick is inserted into the middle and it comes out clean, it's baked.
5. Grate over some more lime zest and enjoy this warm or toasted; it makes a perfect breakfast bread with lots of fresh fruit, yogurt and coffee.

Flapjacks

What is a cookbook without a flapjack recipe? These are what I bake when I get seized by that urgent need for something sweet that's not going to be a big effort and has some goodness in them. These are great to take to work or school in your lunchbox or just to have for a handy snack.

Ingredients
280g/12oz oats, I like Bunalun, but Flahavans are equally fab
70g butter
70g coconut oil
75g honey or golden syrup
75g chopped dates OR raisins
75g mixed chopped nuts
50g/2oz mixed sunflower and pumpkin seeds
1/2 tsp cinnamon
Preheat the oven to 170C/340F/Gas4
Prepare a 20x30cm baking tin or ceramic dish
Makes 16-20 flapjacks, depending on size

Method
1. In a heavy bottomed pot slowly melt the oil, butter and honey or golden syrup together with the cinnamon.
2. Stir in the oats, seeds and nuts and add in the chopped dates or raisins, give everything a good stir.
3. Line a 26cm springform tin, or a baking tray, with baking parchment and pile in the flapjack mixture, pressing it down into the sides of the tin.
4. Bake for 20 minutes until starting to go brown. Allow the flapjacks to cool slightly in the tin before slicing, but do it before they set fully or you won't be able to. Cut them into sizes that suit you.

Yogurt Cake

I made this up one night after giving a class in yogurt making where I arrived home with lots of extra yogurt and a bag of defrosted frozen berries. This is a little bit cheesecake, a little bit sponge, but is made without sugar or any kind of grain, so it's kind to your gut, gluten-free and really delicious too. The coulis keeps in a jar in the fridge for a few weeks, if you want to make it in advance.

Ingredients
For the cake:
250g ground almonds
250g ground coconut
250g yogurt
150g cup honey
Zest of 1 lemon
3 eggs
120g melted butter

For the coulis
500g frozen forest fruit or mixed berries
2-3 tbsp honey

Preheat the oven to 170C/340g/Gas 4
Grease and line the bottom of a 26cm springform tin.

Method
1. First make the coulis: heat up the fruit with the honey in a pot and allowing it to cook for about 5 minutes, then allow this to cool fully.
2. Combine the cake ingredients in a large bowl and mix well using a wooden spoon, no need for a mixer.
3. Pour the cake mix into the prepared tin then drizzle on the coulis and swirl it through the mixture with a cocktail stick.
4. Bake for 50-55 minutes, check to see if it's cooked by inserting a cocktail stick into the centre, if it's clean, the cake is baked. Remove it from the oven and leave it to cool fully before cutting. This cake keeps well for 4-5 days in a tin. You can happily have this for breakfast, it's just fruit and nuts after all.

Autumn Apple Cake

This was the very first recipe I wrote for my blog Val's Kitchen, which I started writing way back in 2006. It was great to put my love of food, writing and taking photos together. I still make this cake regularly as it's so easy and gets tastier over a few days. Over time I've changed some ingredients, but the basic cake is the same, moist and warming and a really comforting treat.

Ingredients

225g butter
450g Bramley apples
Zest and juice of one lemon
225g caster sugar
3 large eggs
225g plain flour OR white spelt flour
2 tsp baking powder
25g ground almonds
1 tbsp brown sugar
Preheat oven to 180°C/ 350F/Gas 4

Method

1. Grease a 28cm springform tin with butter and cut out a circle of greaseproof paper to line the bottom.
2. Peel and chop the apples into small pieces, don't worry about having them uniformly-sized as the apples get very soft in the cake. Squeeze the lemon juice over the apples and give them a stir, leave them aside.
3. Cream the butter in a mixer by whisking it alone for about a minute, then add the sugar and grated lemon zest, beat until it is light in colour and fluffy.
4. Add the eggs, one by one, sifting in some of the flour after each one. Add the baking powder and ground almonds then loosely fold in the apples. Stir the mixture to combine and spoon into the prepared tin. Sprinkle the brown sugar over the top and place in the pre-heated oven.
5. Check the colour after 30 mins. If it is getting too brown cover the cake loosely with tin foil and continue cooking it for a further 20-30 mins. Everybody knows the temperament of their own oven so follow your instincts.
6. Leave the cake to cool in the tin until it's just warm. Be sure to have a slice before it gets cold and smother it with thick, whipped cream. It will keep for a few days in a tin if you can keep your hands off it! If you won't finish it within a week, slice it and wrap the slices in baking parchment, put them in a freezer container and freeze them. This is great when you would go through a wall for something sweet and then remember you have cake in the freezer!

Karen's Cheesy Muffins

Also known as Welsh Rarebit muffins, but the name has been changed, as the first time my friend Karen tasted them, she ate eight of them in one sitting. And so our friendship began! Anyone who says the way to a man's heart is through his stomach clearly doesn't know that women work the same way – everyone can be won over with food. These tangy, cheesy, puffy, savoury treats are great as part of a breakfast or brunch. Slather appropriately with butter when still warm. Muffins are easy, the trick is to mix the dry ingredients in one bowl and all the wet ones in a jug and then pour one into the other and mix them with a fork until just combined. Do NOT use a mixer, or you will get rock buns.

Ingredients
Makes 12

250g wholemeal spelt flour
2 tsp baking powder
1 tsp salt
150g strong cheddar cheese, grated
1 tsp Dijon mustard
50g butter, melted
150g Greek yogurt
125ml milk
1 egg
2 tbsp Worcestershire sauce

Topping

25g grated cheddar
Worcestershire sauce
Preheat the oven to 180C/350F/Gas6

Method

1. Mix the flour, baking powder, salt and cheese in a large mixing bowl with a fork.
2. Mix the remaining ingredients together in a jug and then pour them onto the dry ingredients in the bowl and mix lightly. but thoroughly, with a fork so that everything is just combined.
3. Spoon the puffy mixture into 12 muffin cases in a tin and bake for 20 minutes.
4. Remove the tin from the oven and sprinkle over the remaining cheese, a little on each one and a sprinkling of the Worcestershire sauce. Return them to the oven and bake for a further 5 minutes until the tops are crunchy looking. Butter at the ready, enjoy while they're still warm!

Baked Apples

As a child, I used to turn my nose up at baked apples when my mum made them for dessert. Pity the fool I was, as I missed out on their magical, delicious, toffee transformation in the oven. In autumn, when perfect Bramley cooking apples are practically being given away, you can make these in minutes and throw them in the oven to bake while you're having your dinner.

Serves as many as you like – 1 apple per person

Ingredients

1 good-sized cooking apple per person
1 tbsp dried fruit, raisins or sultanas
1 tbsp runny honey per apple
1 knob butter per apple
Light sprinkling cinnamon
Pouring cream or yogurt to serve
Preheat the oven to 180degreesC/350F/Gas4

Method

1. Wash and core the apples, I use a potato peeler to do this. Pop the apples in an ovenproof dish. If they tend to wobble, simply slice a sliver off their bottoms so they sit upright.
2. Stuff the fruit into the hollow centre and drizzle some honey over – ideally some will dribble down the middle. Sprinkle over a little cinnamon and plop the knob of butter on top.
3. Bake the apples in the oven for 30-40 minutes until the skins crack and everything is golden and oozey. Devour while still warm, with cream or yogurt.

Carrot Cake Muffins

Grain-free, gluten-free, sugar free – and tasty! These easy and deliciously moist muffins tick all the boxes when it comes to a sweet treat that's actually good for you. Have them for breakfast with coffee or as a perfect lunchtime snack. They are also high in protein so make a perfect post-gym snack.

Makes 12

Ingredients

6 free range eggs

120g melted butter or coconut oil

6 tbsp runny honey

1 tbsp vanilla extract

160g coconut flour, you can get this from Asian and health food shops

1 tsp bread soda

1 tsp cinnamon

200g grated carrots

100g raisins or mix of raisins and sultanas

75g chopped walnuts

Preheat the oven to 170C/350F/Gas4

Method

1. Mix the eggs, melted butter or oil, honey and vanilla extract together in a large bowl, then sprinkle in the coconut flour and stir, ensuring you have no lumps. Add the carrots and the remaining ingredients and mix well with a spoon. Don't worry if the mix looks too carroty!

2. Spoon it into muffin cases and bake for 30 minutes or so until they are a nice dark brown.

3. Leave them to cool slightly before devouring. They do stick a little to the papers, so you may need a knife to get off all the sticky bits.

Food

for

Special Days

Let's Go On A Picnic! 🫙

We spent long summers – always hot in my rose-coloured memories – either going on road trips for the day to the seaside or away for a few weeks in West Clare. Along with hordes of cousins, we had epic, long days of adventuring and jumping off sand dunes. The big, red coolbox was packed with boiled eggs, bread and butter, sausage rolls, crisps and plenty of sliced meats to make up salads and sandwiches on the beach. I loved those tinned potato salads, and the intricate assembly of colourful plates of food. Food tastes great when you eat it on the beach, when you're all sandy and spaced out from running in and out of the sea and building sandcastles all day. Since I've become a mum, I've always been quite serious about picnics, sometimes bringing entire dinners in a tiffin tin and a roast chicken to make sure no one went hungry as my lads bobbed for hours in the freezing Atlantic, eventually emerging ravenous. These days I find a stash of fermented treats like pickled beets and sauerkraut can make a great picnic along with a chunk of good cheese and a crusty sourdough loaf; a good knife that cuts bread and tomatoes is an important bit of picnic kit. A few sausage rolls (p117) never go amiss and don't forget the flask of hot water and tea bags and milk in a glass bottle.

For an authentic Irish picnic you will need
Slices of cooked ham, to make 'hang sanniges',
see Phonsie's Ham p118
Coleslaw or Irish sauerkraut p137-8
Pickled beetroot p139

Hard-boiled eggs p29
Baby New Potato Salad
Mixed greens
Tomatoes
Tayto crisps

It's important to arrange everything by placing them side by side on the plate and then let the beetroot make it all pink, just like old times

Baby New Potato Salad

This mix is gorgeous! It tastes great warm or cold.

Ingredients
1kg baby new potatoes
2 tbsp wholegrain mustard
100ml olive oil
Lemon
Salt and black pepper
Parsley and chives, about 2 handfuls

Method
1. Boil or steam the spuds until they are just cooked, take them off the heat and drain them, then crush them lightly and pop them into a large bowl.
2. In a jug mix up the olive oil, lemon and mustard with the salt and pepper and a handful of herbs, pour this over the spuds while they are still warm so that all the flavours get absorbed well.
3. Roughly chop lots of parsley and chives and toss them over the salad and mix loosely, season to taste and enjoy!

Food for Gatherings

Twenty-five years ago, my beautiful sister Anne died of cancer, aged just twenty-three. She was four years older than me. The funeral was a blur, happening over some strangely sunny days in April. Crowds gathered at our house and there was an eternal army of women in the kitchen making tea and buttering bread. Apple tarts appeared on every surface and the generosity of spirit and the kindness of our neighbours and friends is something I will never forget. The feeding was constant, at times when you can't face a meal, an egg salad sandwich can save you, or a sausage roll, or a really great slice of ham on a plate with some coleslaw and potato salad. Nobody bakes a ham like my dad, by the way.

Autumn Apple Cake (p104)

Egg Salad Sandwiches

If you're baking your own sandwich bread, a nice tall white loaf or a lovely springy potato and yeast white loaf will work well, as will an amazing sourdough. On occasions like this, however, bread from a packet does the job; there are some nice granary loaves available. I use spring onion in the sandwich filling as it's milder than regular onion and really makes a difference to the results.

Makes about 24 triangles
Ingredients
6 eggs, hard boiled and peeled
1 medium tomato, finely diced with the seeds removed
6 leaves butterhead lettuce, washed, dried and finely shredded
1 spring onion, finely chopped
Mayonnaise, approx. 2 heaped tbsp, enough to bind
1 loaf of sliced brown or white bread
Butter that's been left out so it's nice and soft, optional

Method
1. In a large bowl mix all the filling ingredients together and season with some salt and pepper.
2. Butter the bread if using butter; I do, it makes then even yummier.
3. Spread enough filling onto a slice of bread and top it with another slice, keep going until the bread or filling, or both are gone. Squish them down a bit and slice diagonally into triangles.
4. If you want to keep these fresh for a couple of hours, soak some greaseproof paper in water, squeeze out any excess, then cover the plates of sandwiches with this, tucking in the edges to keep the air out.

Sausage Rolls

These are the best sausage rolls, and they're so simple and easy. My mum always made them at home before you could buy them frozen and there is a difference, even if they are made with frozen puff pastry they are just delicious and so soothing. Of course you can go nuts with fillings made from minced pork mixed with lamb and deliciously seasoned. But if you find some really great sausages and buy some frozen puff pastry you will still get great results.

Makes 24

Ingredients

100g block frozen puff pastry
12 good-quality pork sausages – the world is your sausage
Egg for brushing and wash
Sesame seeds, for sprinkling
Preheat the oven to 200C/F 375/Gas 6

Method

1. Dust a work surface lightly with some flour to stop everything sticking. Roll out the pastry slowly, moving it around so it doesn't stick, until you have a large square of about 45cm, and about 1/2 cm thick.

2. Peel the skin off the sausages (this is easily done by slipping a fork up one side just inside the sausage skin, and teasing it upwards, the skin will easily open and then peel back). Roll out each sausage a little and place three end to end with no gaps on the pastry square and in about 5cm from the edge, leaving enough pastry to fold over the sausage. You want to fill the length of the square so you may need to add another sausage.

3. Brush some beaten egg along the front of the row of sausages, facing you and roll the pastry over it, pressing the edge down onto the eggy part.

4. Cut the pastry here and, with a fork, pinch the edges together all the way along.

5. Repeat this process until everything is used up. Cut into sausage rolls of whatever size you like, but small is better. Slice a few cuts into the top of each one, brush them all with the beaten egg and sprinkle with sesame seeds..

6. Place the rolls on baking parchment on baking trays and bake them in a hot oven for 15 to 20 minutes until golden. Eat warm, shouldn't be a problem.

Phonsie's Ham

My Dad is famous for his ham so no better man than him to write the recipe, and here it is in his own words:

Tastes vary, but to me nothing quite matches the succulent taste of the original ham, 'smoked' or 'green'. In recent times a number of preferences have developed, such as pouring a can of cider or beer over the ham, or into the roasting dish. Fine, if that's how you prefer it, but not for me. (I can't see me sitting at a bar enjoying my pint, with the barman asking if I would like a rasher of bacon in the glass). No, I'm a bit old-fashioned, but this is how I like it, and it works every time.

Method

1. Whether you go for smoked or green ham is by choice.
2. You've bought your full, or half ham and you're ready to go.
3. Wipe the ham all over with a clean cloth and pop it in a turkey-bag, tie the end of the bag and, with a fork, make a few slits in the bag to allow steam to escape. On to your roasting dish and into the cold oven.
4. Set the oven temp to 180C/350F/GAS4.
5. Cooking time for a 7kg ham will be about 4 hours including heating up time.
6. Adjust downwards for a half ham, about 2 ½ hours.
7. After about 3½ hours remove the ham from the oven and cut open the bag and remove the ham onto a large platter; you'll need help with this, it's very hot, and heavy. Pour the liquid hot fat into a bowl (it's not needed any longer).
8. Remove the outer layer of fat from the ham and decorate with some cloves, about 8cms apart over the upper surface of the meat. Back into the oven,
9. 140C/280F/Gas2 for about 15 minutes, then remove.
10. While all this has been going on, a few slices of white bread were toasting on a spare shelf in the oven, and when nice and crisp, crushed with the rolling pin.
11. The toasty crumbs are patted all over the surface of the ham.
12. Job done. Can't wait for a few slices.

Happy Birthday To You!

Birthday parties are a day of celebration and you don't want to be worried about kids going nuts on too much sugar. I've always done my kids' parties at home mainly for reasons of economics, but also because the stuff that gets passed off as 'food' in some playparks doesn't bear thinking about. All bets are off on birthdays really, who wants to be all healthy and virtuous? But strewing a table with chocolate bars and fizzy drinks isn't the only option either. You want happy kids who actually get something to eat, but who aren't so wired that they are swinging from the chandeliers. Two things that everybody loves are fried chicken and pizza. Of course you have to have decadent chocolate brownies (p98) and perfect fizzy drinks (p124).

The soda bread pizza recipe here can be made on a frying pan or in the oven – better still you can clear off a big table and get the kids to make their own pizzas, something that pizza restaurants charge big money for. The fried chicken is easy and you can make it all ahead of time and reheat it in the oven or enjoy it just as much cold. Cooking the chicken in water first ensures it is fully cooked and you also get left with a yummy chicken stock.

Fried Chicken

Makes 10 pieces

Ingredients

1 free range chicken
1 carrot
1 stick celery
A bay leaf and sprig of thyme
2 garlic cloves, chopped
2 eggs
Flour, for coating the chicken
1/2 tsp sweet or smoked paprika
Salt and pepper
Light olive oil, for frying

Method

1. Joint the chicken into legs, thighs, wings and breast on the bone portions, cut the breast portion into 2 pieces.
2. Pop all the chicken, including the carcass, into a large pot with the carrot, celery and herbs and a little salt, bring it to a boil and turn down the heat to simmer and cook for 15 minutes.
3. Remove the chicken pieces from the pot and leave them to drain.
4. Mix the chopped garlic with the eggs and coat the chicken with this mixture; leave to marinate in the fridge for at least an hour or overnight.
5. Heat up enough olive oil in a deep frying pan to fry the chicken.
6. Mix the flour with the salt, pepper and paprika. Drain the chicken pieces from the marinade, coat them in the flour mixture and fry in batches until golden. Remove from the oil onto kitchen paper and drain.

Soda Bread Pizza

You can make this on a heavy-bottomed frying pan, but if you're making a large quantity then the oven is better. What makes this recipe so good is that you don't need to spend ages waiting for yeast dough to rise.

Ingredients
500g plain/white spelt flour
1 tsp bread soda
1 tsp salt
375ml buttermilk

Toppings
Grated cheese
Tomato purée
Sliced pepper, salami, pineapple, mushrooms for toppings

Method

1. Make up your soda bread by putting the flour, bread soda and salt into a large bowl and mixing with your hand. Pour in the buttermilk and, using your hand like a claw, bring it all together to form a loose dough. Turn it out onto a floured surface and bring the dough together into a ball. Divide it into 2, or 4 if you are making your pizzas on the frying pan.

2. Take one ball and roll it out into a circle less than 1cm thick that fits onto your frying pan – don't oil the pan – pop the dough on and let it brown, this should take about 5 minutes.

3. Meanwhile slice your peppers, mushrooms and anything you are using as toppings.

4. When the pizza base has nice golden patches, flip it over.

5. Spread some tomato purée over the top of the base and lay on your toppings and cheese while the underside cooks.

6. Now pop it under a hot grill for a few minutes to make everything nice and bubbly.

7. Slide the pizza out onto a board and cut into slices, enjoy your Irish/Italian fusion creation!

In the Pantry

Delicious Drinks

Note: all bottles used to make the drinks should be sterilised. See p 137.

Elderflower 'Champagne'

The best time of year to pick the pretty elderflowers is June or July when the flowers are a gorgeous pale cream colour with a strong scent. It's fun to go gallivanting over ditches and definitely a good idea to pick them away from busy roads – you don't want them loaded with car fumes. Bring a strong scissors or secateurs and somebody to help you with high up branches, where, inevitably, all the best ones are. Whatever you leave behind, you can come back for in autumn when you want to make your elderberry cordial.

Ingredients
1kg sugar
Flowers from 10 elderflower sprays
Grated zest and juice of 4 lemons
½ tsp yeast, maybe, maybe not
You will need: 10x 500ml bottles with flip top lids, a clean plastic bucket, a funnel and some muslin for straining

Method
1. Dissolve the sugar in a clean plastic bucket in 2 litres of boiled, hot water. Top up with 3 more litres of water and leave to cool.
2. Add the lemon zest and juice, and the elderflowers (give them a shake to remove any forest creatures). Stir and cover with a cloth.
3. Check the mix after 3 days and if there is no sign of bubbles, sneak in your yeast and give it a stir. Cover again and leave for 3 more days
4. Strain the mix through muslin into a clean container and leave it settle for a few minutes before bottling it into your cooled sterilised bottles. Close the lids and store the bottles at room temperature for a week before drinking.
5. Using bottles that are really airtight here is key. (The big ones you can buy full of pink lemonade are perfect). Elderflower champagne can be explosive so it's a good idea to store the bottles away from people and open carefully! This will store for months in a cool, dark place; bear in mind alcohol content will rise as fermentation goes on.

Cordials

Cordials are a great way of storing the vivid flavours of free food in season. This method of preserving also keeps all the vitamin C intact so these drinks are lifesavers in winter; I wouldn't be without my stash of elderberry or rosehip cordial to ward off colds. I once ran a mini microbrewery called 'The Elder Lemon'; I designed and made my own labels and was supplying three shops in Limerick with yummy lemon, rhubarb and elderflower cordials. Making small batches of cordials at home is easy and rewarding.

Elderflower Cordial

Makes 10 x 500ml bottles

Ingredients

40-ish elderflower heads/sprays

4 unwaxed lemons, zest and juice

1 kg sugar

Method

1. Place the elderflowers in a bucket, first shaking off any insects, add the lemon zest. Pour boiling water over the flowers, cover with a cloth and leave them to infuse overnight.

2. Line a strainer with muslin and pour some boiling water through it. Strain the elder into a large pot and add the sugar, bring it to a boil and simmer for 5 minutes.

3. Have your bottles freshly sterilised and, ideally, still hot and carefully funnel the syrup into them and pop the lids on. Dilute this to taste and have it with plain water, fizzy water or diluted in a glass of prosecco!

Elderberry Cordial

Elderberries are the mature version of elderflowers, handsome deep-purplish berries, quite alluring and vampy, in season around September. Pick them ripe, but not wrinkly, cut at the stem, then 'comb' the berries off the stems with a fork or your fingers until you have nothing but berries.

Makes about 4 x 500ml bottles

Ingredients

1kg elderberries, rinsed of small creatures

Sugar (see below for quantity)

Cloves, optional, but they do add a nice depth

Method

1. Put the elderberries into a large pot and just cover them with water (if a few green ones rise to the surface, get rid of them). Bring to the boil, reduce the heat, leave to simmer for 20 minutes.
2. Line a large strainer with muslin and sit it over a big bowl. Pour the cooked berries in. Leave to strain and then squeeze out the squidgy mess, getting out as much liquid as you can.
3. Measure the juice and pour it back into the rinsed pot. For each 500ml of juice add 300g sugar and 4 cloves.
4. Bring the mixture to the boil and simmer for 10 minutes.
5. Have your sterilised, and preferably still hot, bottles at the ready. Pour the syrup into the bottles (be careful doing this and have someone to help you by holding the funnel and bottles in place), pop the lids on and wipe them down with a damp cloth. Reward yourself by pouring some syrup into a glass and topping up with fizzy water, ice and a sprig of mint!

Rosehip Syrup

Rosehips, also called haws, are said to be the most concentrated form of Vitamin C.

Ingredients

500g rosehips, topped and tailed (this means cutting off their fuzzy ends and stems)
1 1/2 litre water
500g sugar

Method

1. Put the rosehips into a food processor or blender and roughly chop.
2. Put them into a pot with 2 pints of water and bring to a boil, lower the heat and simmer for 15 minutes.
3. Line a strainer with muslin and pour the mixture into this, leave it strain for about an hour then give it a good squeeze. Return the rosehips to the pot with another pint of water and repeat the process.
4. You should now have about 1 litre of rosehip juice. Rinse out your pot and reheat the juice with 500g sugar and bring it to a boil. Simmer the mixture for 5 minutes.
5. Pour the hot syrup into the hot bottles and pop the lids on. This will store for months; be sure to take some any time a cold hits you.

Lemonade Cordial

Makes 2 x 500ml bottles
Ingredients
7-10 unwaxed lemons
500g sugar
Water

Method

1. Bring a large pot of water to a boil. Zest the lemons and add the zest to the water. When it's boiling, add the lemons and boil them for 1 minute. Boiling the lemons will release almost twice the amount of juice.
2. Strain the water and keep 500ml of it and return it to the pan with 500ml of the lemon juice and 700g sugar. Bring this to a boil and cook it for a minute to ensure the sugar is dissolved.
3. Pour the cordial into hot, sterilised bottles and cork immediately. When it's cooled enjoy this over ice or fizzy water for a real American-style traditional lemonade.

Rhubarb Cordial

If there was ever a drink to enchant you, the beautiful, dusky, antique pink of this rhubarb drink is it. When you taste it, nothing comes close to its cheeky, tart flavour. This goes well with water, fizzy water, champagne and with gin.

Sterilise 2 x500ml bottles
Ingredients
1 1/2kg rhubarb cleaned and chopped into chunks
1kg (approx) sugar
2-3 lemons
You will need some muslin and a stick/broom handle and string to drain the liquid

Method

1. Put the rhubarb in a pot with 100ml water and bring to a boil. Turn down the heat and simmer slowly for about 40 minutes until the fruit is very soft.
2. Line a large strainer with muslin, over a large bowl and tip the rhubarb mush into it, letting it drain. When the dripping has mostly stopped, tie the bag with string at the top and suspend it over the bowl, ensuring that it doesn't touch the juice. Leave this overnight if possible, draping over a tea-towel to keep it clean.
3. The next day measure the juice; for every litre, add 700g sugar and 50ml lemon juice and reheat this in a pot until the sugar is dissolved. Bottle your cordial and enjoy it diluted with 3 parts water for a sophisticated summer drink that's full of vitamins.

Cider

Ireland has a perfect climate to grow apples and a long history in apple growing, with some wild and wonderful names like Bloody Butcher, Widow's Friend and Ahearne Beauty; wouldn't you want to do something with them? This homemade cider is refreshing and only mildly alcoholic, though the longer you leave it the stronger and drier it gets. Otherwise it is an invigorating and delicious drink from nature.

Ingredients
2 dozen sweet apples, preferably unsprayed, washed
1 tsp sea salt
50ml whey (see pp 137)
You need: a juicer, a sterilised 2 litre jar and some muslin.

Method
1. Pass the apples through a juicer, pausing to remove the pulp after every 10 apples or so, otherwise it will clog. Skim off the foam and discard or compost it.
2. Pour the juice into your jar and add the salt and whey and give it a stir, cover with muslin and leave at room temperature for 3-4 days. In winter it's better to put this in the hot press or somewhere of about 20-22 degrees C.
3. Remove from the hot press and bottle into cooled, sterile bottles. This gets very fizzy indeed so store it in the fridge for at least a day before you want to drink it or you may lose all your drink to the 'geyser effect'.

Apple Cider Vinegar

It's said that a spoonful of cider vinegar every day can relieve everything from arthritis to osteoporosis. It soothes burns, helps cure a sore throat, chases away flu symptoms, eases sunburn and is a great aid to digestion. Some lovers of cider vinegar claim that drinking a spoonful every morning gets them set up for the day, it promotes a feeling of fullness so it can aid weight management too.

Method
1. To make this, simply leave your cider under its muslin cover for up to 4 weeks. Being exposed to the air will let all the gasses subside and the cider will ferment into vinegar and become flat. You can now bottle it and store it for several months.

Dairy

During my childhood I remember cheese as two things; one was a blue box with a cute smiley girl on it – Calvita cheese. The other one was a thing called Easi Singles (a good name for a dating website!), which were orange, square things wrapped so tightly in plastic that you could think the plastic was part of the 'cheese'. Back when Ireland joined the EU, farmers were being encouraged to add value to their milk by turning it into cheese, otherwise it paid them more to pour the milk down the fields. Happily this resulted in a stratospheric turnaround in Irish cheese-making; we are now up there beside and beyond some of the best-known cheese-producing countries. As we have so much rain, we have the best pasture and therefore the best dairy for making cheese and other dairy products.

On the beautiful Beara Peninsula I was lucky enough to meet a legend of cheese-making, Veronica Steele who has been making Mileen's Cheese since the late seventies. I cooked her scrambled eggs for her breakfast and she commented, 'They weren't bad at all', especially as we had put some of her own cheese on top. According to Veronica 'Any fool can make a cheese, but it takes a genius to ripen it.' As making these simple cheeses requires little in terms of kitchen gadgets, I was keen to give it a try. I always use unpasteurised milk for my yogurt and cheese adventures as it contains all the good bacteria and results in smoother, better tasting results.

Easy Cream Cheese

Special things needed: Cheesecloth/muslin 1 metre, available from cookery or hardware shops. You will have to scald this by pouring boiling water over it so put the kettle on.

It's a good habit to get into, to have everything you use as clean as possible by boiling your utensils in hot water first, don't use any detergent as this will leave residue.

Ingredients
1 litre raw milk or regular milk, full fat only

Method
1. Pour the milk into a squeaky-clean glass container and cover loosely with a clean tea towel. Leave at room temperature for 3-4 days until the milk separates, in winter I put mine in the hot press. You will know it's ready as the milk will be wobbly if you shake the bowl.

2. Line a clean strainer (that will fit over another clean bowl) with two layers of scalded muslin, and pour in the set milk, cover this loosely again with a tea towel. Leave it to drip into the bowl for several hours and then gather up the extra cloth and tie it to a wooden spoon or stick and hang it over the bowl to continue dripping for 24 hours at least. Do not squeeze it. (Don't tie it from the beginning, if you do, you get a very runny centre.)

3. When it has stopped dripping the cream cheese is ready and the whey that has dripped into the bowl can be stored for later use. Whey is a powerful probiotic in itself and can be used a starter culture for many fruit and vegetable ferments.

Cheese Balls

You will need a sterilised jar to keep your cheeseballs in.

Use as much of your cream cheese as you like for this recipe, the amounts here are guidelines

Ingredients

200g homemade cream cheese
50g freshly-ground black pepper and / or ground dilisk
100ml light olive oil

Method

1. Take a spoonful of your cream cheese and roll into a ball, using wet hands, then roll the little balls in freshly-ground black pepper or ground dilisk. Store them in a light olive oil and enjoy their bursting freshness alone or spread on some crunchy sourdough toast.

Paneer

This is the easiest and fastest cheese you can make. Paneer is an Indian cheese usually made from buffalo milk that has a hard, almost rubbery texture. It stands up to frying and so it can be used in curry dishes and it retains its shape. It can be marinated

in herbs and garlic, as I like to do as the cheese has no added salt. You can add some salt to the curds while making it if you like.

Ingredients
1 litre raw milk or regular milk, full fat only
Juice of 1 lemon
1/2 tsp sea salt

Method
1. Heat the milk in a pot, bring it to a foamy boil. Stir the milk and pour in the lemon juice, turn off the heat and continue stirring until clumps of curd start to appear.
2. Keep stirring the milk until you have large clumps.
3. Now sit a colander over a bowl and line it with muslin or cheesecloth which you have scalded. Pour the cheesy mixture into the cloth and let most of the liquid drain (this whey has lemon in it so don't keep it to use in other recipes, but it tastes great as a warming drink), sprinkle on your salt, if using and give the curds a little stir.
4. Now fold over the cheesecloth and sit a heavy weight on top of the cheese, I use a marble mortar and pestle. Within about half an hour your cheese is ready. Ta, da!

Yogurt
Yogurt is bursting with beneficial bacteria that are great for your gut flora. It can be added to smoothies or nutola to make a substantial breakfast or anytime snack. The easiest starter to get you going is a live probiotic yogurt. Old McDonald's is widely available and does the job nicely. Using raw milk instead of commercial will give you a a sweeter yogurt. If you want to retain as much of the milk's good bacteria, then the first method of making the yogurt will do that, it will probably result in a runnier yogurt however. It's worth investing in a milk thermometer for this.

Ingredients

1 litre cows' or goats' raw or organic milk, full fat only

50g live probiotic natural yogurt (standard natural yogurt works well too just be sure it isn't a thickened variety)

Preheat the oven to 180C/350F/Gas4

Method

1. Heat the milk in a clean pan until just below 180F/80C degrees, use a thermometer for this.

2. Remove the pan from the heat and sit it into a basin of cold water and allow it to cool to about 36C/110F.

3. Stir in the 2 tbsp yogurt and cover the pan with a clean tea towel.

4. Turn off the oven and place the pot into it, leave it overnight, or put the lid on the pot and wrap it in towel and put it in the hotpress overnight. The point is that you want to incubate it. In the morning, or at least 8 hours later, you will have deliciously smooth and creamy yogurt. Alternatively pour the mixture into a clean thermos flask that you have just heated up with some boiling water and leave it overnight. You might want to keep a thermos just for this purpose.

5. Keep the yogurt in sterilised, clean jars or a tub in the fridge and use within the week. This yogurt can be used in lots of other recipes and of course is the perfect starter for your next batch.

Thick Set Yogurt

This yogurt has a more set consistency and it very easy to make too. You need the same ingredients as above.

Method

1. Bring the milk to a boil and let it reduce by one third by leaving it to simmer. Take it off the heat and transfer it into a clean glass bowl or a wide mouthed glass jar and allow it to cool until the temperature is like your own body temperature, about 36C/110F.

2. Stir in the yogurt, cover the bowl with a plate or put the lid on loosely, cover this with a cloth and leave it overnight in the hot-press or a cooling oven again for the night.

3. In the morning you will have a gorgeous smooth and thick creamy yogurt.

Fabulous Ferments: Listen to your Gut

Fermenting or 'canning' foods is one of the oldest methods of food preservation and can keep food tasting fresh and crunchy for months or even years. From German sauerkrauts (pickled vegetables), from beer and wine to dried meats like salamis and chorizo, people all around the world have fermented foods to make them last. In Ireland, traditionally we enjoyed fermented foods like buttermilk, a by-product of butter making; mead was made by letting honey ferment with water and, on the Aran Islands, they fermented sharks' liver to use as a superfood to supplement their basic diets. Getting into fermenting is as easy as salting some cabbage and putting it in a jar.

Eating fermented foods will raise your energy levels by improving your digestion and they will boost your immune system too as they contain powerful probiotics. Eat a little, even a teaspoon a day, of your chosen ferments and add more gradually until you find you just can't imagine a meal without them. Happy fermenting!

Fermenting: getting started

Things to have:

Glass jars and bottles (it's worth getting good jars and bottles; Kilner last well, have replaceable rubber seals and they look great. You could also wash flip-top beer bottles for your fizzy drinks or screw top wine bottles for cordials.)
Muslin
Plastic strainer
A large plastic bowl or two

Sterilise your equipment:

Cleanliness is key if you want your ferments and cordials to keep a long time. To sterilise bottles or jars simply put them through a wash cycle in the dishwasher, but without a tablet as this leaves chemical residue. You can also wash and rinse your glassware and then cook them at 160C/320F/Gas 3 for 10 minutes OR boil everything in a large pot of water for 10 minutes. I boil the lids and rubber seals in a pot as you cannot put these in the oven.

Whey

Whey can be made by tipping the contents of a tub of natural yogurt into a muslin lined strainer and leave it to strain for a few hours. You can then enjoy a delicious thick yogurt and store your whey for months.

Note: all jars mentioned in recipes below should be sterlisised (see above).

Sauerkraut and other krauts

Sauerkraut is a staple in German homes and has been adapted the world over as a miraculous, health-giving food that is easy and cheap to make. This version is so refreshing compared to shop-bought versions and goes well with cheese and cold meats.

Equipment needed: 1 x 1litre mason jar, 1 instrument for 'pounding' the cabbage like a flat-ended rolling pin, a very clean, large plastic basin or bowl, a small jar or stone for weighing the cabbage down in the jar (this will also have to be sterilised by scrubbing it and boiling it for one hour). You can also use a patented Sterilock.

Makes one 1-litre jar

Ingredients

1 head organic cabbage, red or white

1 tsp sea salt

4 tbsp whey (as an alternative to whey you can just use an extra tsp salt)

1 tsp caraway seeds or other flavourings like star anise or black peppercorns

Method

1. Shred the cabbage with a large knife; you can use a food processor, but it tends to chop the cabbage too finely.

2. Put the cabbage into the bowl with the salt and whey, if using. Mix everything together with your hands and then get your rolling pin or stick and begin pounding the cabbage; keep going for 10 minutes until some of the juices are released. Sprinkle on the caraway seeds or other flavourings, if using.

3. Get your sterile jar, pack the cabbage in, including the juices, then press everything down with your stick and pop in your small jar or stone to put pressure on the cabbage when you close the lid. You want the cabbage to be submerged in the juices; it should be almost 3cm from the top of the jar. If your cabbage doesn't fill the jar enough, you will have too much oxygen in the jar and it will spoil. Place the jar on a plate to catch any juices that overflow.

4. Leave the jar at room temperature (18-20C) for 4-5 days. You should see bubbles inside, this means it's fermenting! Open the jar every day to release the gases. The carbon dioxide being released may make the jar spit juices at you, so be prepared; always keep the jars on a plate or tray when fermenting to catch any spillages. Once the bubbles have died down, you can remove the small weight inside and store the jar somewhere unheated or in the fridge where it should keep happily for months.

5. For an Irish kraut variation, simply add two grated carrots and a couple of shredded spring onions (to give you green white and orange) to the cabbage and continue as above for a light, salady ferment.

Fermented Veggies

I love teaching this in my classes – no one can ever believe it's so easy. The colours in layers look so pretty too and this transforms ordinary veggies into delicious, crunchy superfood powerhouses.

Ingredients

One cauliflower, broken into small florets
2-3 large carrots, washed and scraped/peeled and cut into sticks of about 3cm thick
1-3 tsp sea salt or 1 tsp sea salt and 1 tbsp whey
1 litre spring/filtered/boiled water (cooled)
You will need a 2-litre jar/any decent sized jar to get started

Method

1. Prepare and wash your veg in clean, ideally filtered or cooled boiled water.
2. In a clean jug dissolve the salt or salt and whey in the water.
3. Layer the veggies tightly in your jar, leaving a space or about 2cm at the top of the jar.
4. Pour over the water mixture, just enough to barely cover them, and press the veggies down with a small jar/weight, and close the jar. Put the jar on a plate and leave it at room temperature for 3-4 days, letting the gasses escape once a day. Once the gases have subsided you can remove the weight in the jar and transfer it to cold storage. Fermented vegetables like this make a great addition to a picnic and you will quickly develop a taste for their tangy, tart flavours

Pickled Beetroot

Who remembers Irish summers with the classic salad of ham, corned beef, a sliced boiled egg, some potato salad from a tin (which I loved), lettuce, tomato, a handful of Taytos and, to top it all, a few slices of that dubious pickled beetroot that mingled with the salad cream and eventually turned everything on the plate a wild pink colour? Here's a recipe that brings that nostalgia back! Easy, fun, and delicious.

Ingredients

6 large beetroot/12 medium
1 litre filtered water
2 tsp sea salt or

1 tsp sea salt and 2 tbsp whey
Preheat the oven to 150C/320F/Gas 3
You will need a 1.5l jar

Method

1. Place the unpeeled beetroot on a roasting tray and bake them for 3 hours until a knife goes in easily. Remove the tray from the oven and leave them to cool.

2. Peel the beets and slice them into slices or sticks about 2cm thick and place the beets in your clean jar, leaving a space of about 2.5cm from the top. Press them down firmly with your hand or a spoon.

3. Mix all the remaining ingredients together and pour them over the beets, giving the liquid time to mingle through all the spaces. Make sure the beets are just covered and seal your jar.

4. Place it in a warm spot, ideally 20-22C degrees and leave it for 4-5 days, checking once a day and releasing the gases by opening the jar. When the bubbles have subsided, pop the jar in the fridge and enjoy with your retro summer salads.

Beetroot Kvass

As this is made with whey from your cheese or yogurt making, kvass is practically a free drink that's fantastic for promoting good digestive health. It's a tonic for the blood, liver and kidneys and helps regularity. It's also quite tasty as the fermentation brings out the sweetness of the beetroot and it becomes slightly effervescent. Kvass takes on a beautiful, purple colour and has a refreshing, sweet and salty flavour.

Ingredients

1 large beetroot, uncooked, organic will work best here
1 cup whey
1 tbsp sea salt
Filtered/spring water, enough to fill the jar
You will need 1 x 2-3 litre glass jar

Method

1. Simply peel and slice the beetroot into chunky chips and place them in the jar, topping up with the whey, salt and water until the jar is almost full.

2. Keep the jar at room temperature for 2-3 days and then transfer somewhere cool, ideally the fridge, but if you live in Ireland, any storage that's unheated in winter will do.

3. Drink a glass in the morning, diluted with water if you prefer, and one in the evening. This is a great tonic for your liver and said to help with joint pain too.

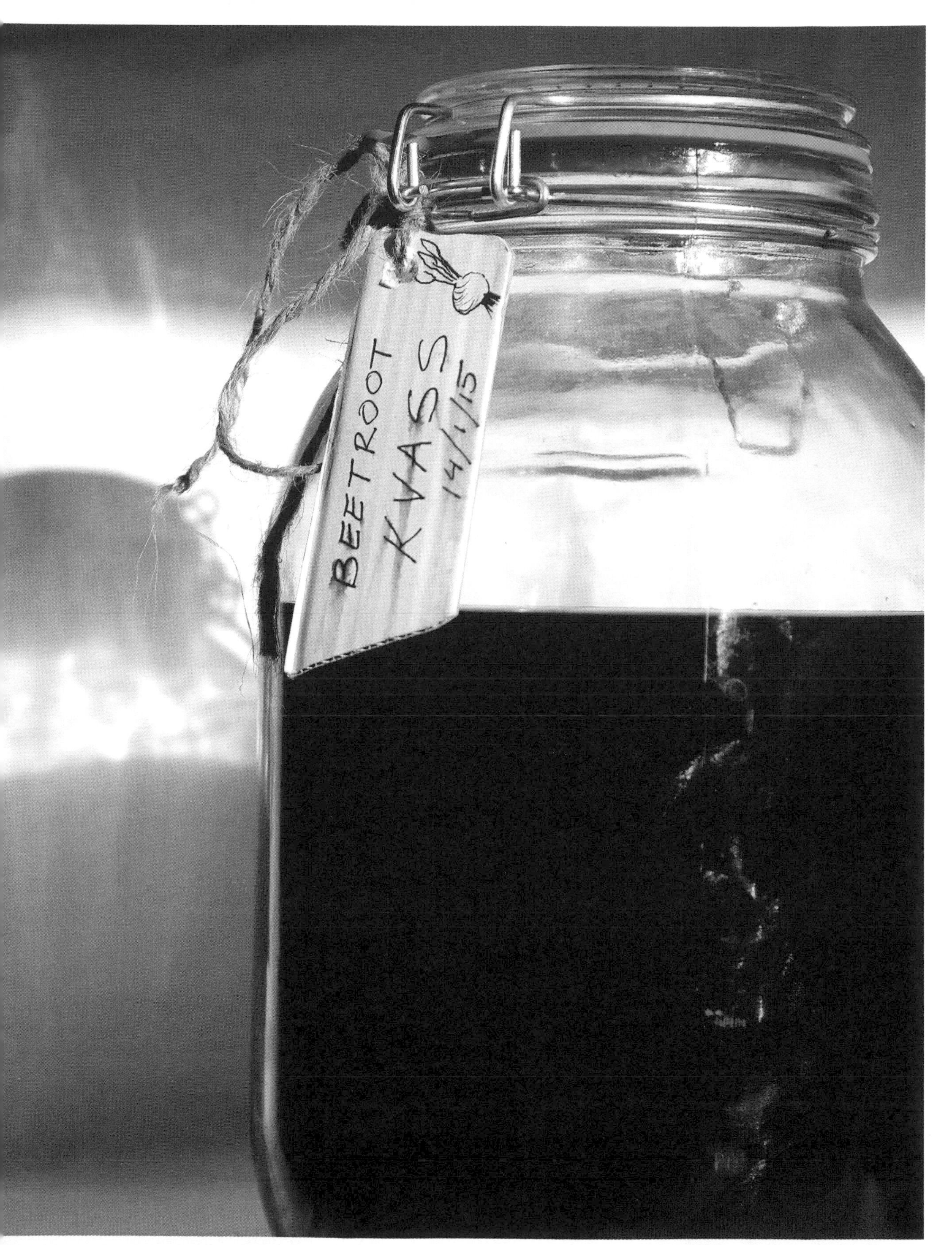
BEETROOT
KVASS
14/1/15

4. When the jar is almost empty of liquid, top it up again with fresh water and leave it at room temperature for 2-3 days and repeat the process until the colour goes out of the water. Then begin a new batch from scratch.

Kimchi

Said to be one of the healthiest foods in the world, kimchi is easy to make and ferments quickly, plus its tangy spiciness is strangely addictive.

Ingredients
2 napa or Chinese cabbages, cut into quarters lengthways and then into chunks
8 tbsp sea salt
4 spring onions, cut into pieces about 3cm long
4 tbsp Korean chilli powder
4 tbsp fish sauce
100g fresh ginger, peeled and grated
6-8 medium garlic cloves, finely chopped
You will need a 2-litre glass mason jar, a large plastic bowl and tongs

Method
1. Wash the cabbage and discard the middle spine, place it in a large plastic bowl and sprinkle over the sea salt. Cover with water until the cabbage is submerged and weigh it down with a dinner plate, for leave at least 4 hours and up to 24 hours to soak.
2. Strain off the water and rinse the cabbage under cold, running water, squeeze out as much excess water as you can and return the cabbage to the rinsed bowl.
3. In another bowl mix the remaining ingredients and pour this over the cabbage, mix everything well to combine it and now pack it into your clean jar, pressing it all down as you go.
4. Get your small jar or weight and pop it on top of the cabbage, you should be able to slowly lever the jar closed. It's important that the cabbage remains submerged in the liquid. Place the jar on a plate and leave at room temperature.
5. After 2-3 days you should see some activity in the form of bubbles, open the jar to let any gasses out and close it again, repeat this for up to six days when the kimchi should ready to put in the fridge. The fridge will stop the fermentation process and make your snack even tastier.

Fermented Baked Beans

Fermenting beans is an easy way to make your own baked beans that you can then store in sealed jars and whip them out when you are hungry for a snack; they come in handy just heated up with a pile of mature cheddar cheese on top for a quick lunch.

Ingredients

500g dried white beans, like haricots
2 tbsp whey
Water, enough to cover the beans
1 250ml jar passata
1 tbsp white wine/cider vinegar
1 tsp sea salt
1 tsp smoked paprika
2 bay leaves
1 spring fresh thyme and rosemary
50g butter or duck fat
2 tbsp honey

Method

1. Leave the beans to soak overnight in cold water. The next day strain them and top up with fresh water, add the whey and give it a stir. Cover loosely and leave everything to ferment for 6-7 days.
2. Preheat the oven to 180C/350F/Gas4.
3. Strain and rinse the beans and put them into a large casserole with a tight-fitting lid with the remaining ingredients and enough water to ensure they are covered, give everything a stir. Bring the pot to a bubble on top of the cooker and then pop on a tight-fitting lid and transfer it to the oven to bake at the high temperature for 15 mins, then reduce the heat to 150C for 3-4hours. Check the beans occasionally to make sure they aren't drying out.
4. To store the beans, sterilise some jars by boiling them for 10 minutes or putting them through the dishwasher. Fill up the hot jars with the hot beans and pop the lids on tightly. These will keep for up to a year if stored in the fridge.

Preserved Lemons

This recipe makes a lively, punchy condiment that goes really well with fish and Middle Eastern dishes.

Ingredients

8-10 lemons, ideally unwaxed
4-5 tbsp sea salt
Sprig rosemary
1 fresh red or green chilli
You will need a one litre jar

Method

1. Juice four of the lemons and set aside.
2. Spilt the remaining ones almost down to their base by cutting a cross in them from the top.
3. Hold the lemons over the jar and stuff them with a tablespoon each of the sea salt
4. Pack them into the jar as tightly as you can.
5. Push in the rosemary and chilli and top up with enough lemon juice to almost cover the lemons.
6. Close the jar and leave in a dark place (about 20C); I find the kitchen an ideal place. The lemons will get quite effervescent so open the jar daily to let out the gases. They will be ready to eat once the bubbles have subsided; this normally takes about a week. Keep in the fridge and use as needed, their flavour will continue to improve over time. To use the lemons, remove one from the jar and rinse off the excess salt, chop as chunky or as fine as you like.

Grow it Yourself

Growing Your Own Food

One of the most satisfying things you can do as as cook is to grow a few things yourself. It will give you an appreciation for the price of that bunch of organic carrots being sold by the small farmer, or that bag of salad leaves with so much flavour and texture compared to the nitrate-filled one in the supermarket. As someone without a garden (but who studied organic horticulture for two years) I am qualified to lecture about not needing a patch of land to grow food, but if you do have one, you are lucky.

Any food you involve your kids in growing will be hoovered up by them. I have a flat roof where I grow spuds in shopping bags, peas in pots, onions, spring onions, herbs, broccoli in window boxes, tomatoes in hanging baskets, garlic, strawberries, raspberries, runner beans, peas, salad leaves and on it goes. To be on that roof of a summer's eve with my young sons, nibbling on fresh peas out of the pot and sampling spinach leaves was a fun and sweet time, they would never have eaten those things if they hadn't seen them growing.

Gardening and putting your hands in the soil has been proven to reduce symptoms of depression, not just because you are outside and doing something, but because the soil contains hormones that boost seratonin production, so you can really get a buzz from sowing, planting, preparing the ground and harvesting your efforts. Just growing a few herbs in window boxes will take your cooking to another level and add bursts of iron and vitamin C to your daily routine. Convinced? Good, let's get growing.

Organic produce costs more as it has to be grown by humans and has to be grown in the soil, as opposed to many crops that are now grown in water or 'hydroponically'. Organic food is fed with organic matter/humus and keeps the cycle of life going with the worms, bugs and nature doing the work she is intended to do. It's so easy to grow a few, or a lot of, edible plants from herbs in a window box to soft fruits and vegetables. It's a good idea to grow what you like to eat, simple.

Given that you might just have space for a few containers let's begin with a basic herb garden, as these are the things that will take your cooking from meh to marvelous. Throw some chopped chives and chive flowers onto your scrambled eggs, sprinkle some oregano on roasted tomatoes, thyme on baked mushrooms, parsley on just about anything. Herbs bring your food to life and inject a hefty dose of vitamins and minerals into your meals.

Herbalicious

People often buy pots of herbs in supermarkets and take them home and wonder why they die. These pots are usually grown intensively in hot houses and will die of shock in your steamy or freezing kitchen. Get past this problem by instantly re-potting them in a larger pot with some fresh compost and watering them. If they look wilty, give them a haircut, this can revive them very well.

These hardy perennials will grow for many years and can be your constant kitchen companions:

Thyme - tasty and fragrant, great in stuffing, chicken dishes and makes a soothing tea for a chesty cough.

Bayleaf - fragrant and distinct, one or two leaves are great in a casserole, don't overdo it.

Rosemary - lamb's best friend, lay a shoulder on top of a bed of rosemary and garlic and roast for 2 1/2 hours, yum.

Oregano - great in anything Italian, crush some skinned and seeded tomatoes and mix with oregano, olive oil and salt for a delicious and fresh tomato concasse, throw on a pizza.

Mint, chocolate mint, pineapple mint are all beasts and will come back year after year and will spread like crazy so keep them contained in pots or containers or make a mint bed if you're partial to a few mojitos. A mint tea will soothe a dodgy tummy and helps digestion.

Chives come back year after year, they are delicious on scrambled eggs and their purple flowers go amazingly well with paté.

Parsley grows for two years before needing to be replaced but it is strong and takes a bit of cold weather.

Other herbs like basil, coriander and dill are more delicate and suited to hot climates. You may have success growing these indoors or in a sheltered, sunny spot.

Cut back the hardy herbs after every growing season by giving the the 'Chelsea chop', a good haircut that cuts them down to about 15cm. This will ensure they don't get woody and become more tree than herb.

If you want to plant a herby window box, drainage is key. Ensure there are drainage holes in the box and throw in a few broken up pieces of crockery or some stones or a mixture, follow this with your soil or compost. If you have been composting at home then mix a little bit of this in with the soil.

Make spaces where you want your plants to be and take them out of their pots, loosening up their roots and popping them into the spaces you have made for them. Add in some more soil and flatten everything down, water the plants in well.

If you can devote a patch of your garden or a bed to herbs this is a great investment of space and it will surprise you every year.

Cooking essentials

Its amazing how many dishes are dependent on onions and garlic for flavour. Try making a curry or a stew or soup without starting off by slowly cooking an onion in some butter or oil and you will end up with a tasteless dish with no depth or warmth to it. Curries naturally thicken when onions meet tomatoes or yogurt. Onions are great for any coughs or colds and have all manner of magical detoxing properties.

Onions

Growing your own onions requires a bit of space that you can devote just to them as they will sit in the soil for months. However it is so easy so if you can do it, do.

Onion sets (little onions) can be bought from after christmas in garden shops. Prepare your soil (see below) and ensure it is raked over or at least that it doesn't have any big lumps of soil and rock. Press the onions sets (bulbs) into the soil at a space of about 6 inches apart, leaving the pointy end sticking out. Birds do love new onions so its a good idea to net them. Onions are ready when their stalks fall over. Carefully lift them from the soil and brush off any excess dirt, dry them and store.

Shallots

Shallots are amazing because you plant one little bulb and it miraculously turns into a whole bulb of onions while your back is turned.

Shallots will grow well in a window box as they are happy in shallow ground, and you can plant them straight into the soil too. Simply pop the seeds (called sets) about 15cm apart with the tops just sticking out of the ground.

When the sets have become a magic hand-full they are ready to harvest. Just lift them from the ground, dry them off on a bright window sill and store them to use when you want a more delicate onion flavour.

Spring Onions

Spring onions or scallions are a great introduction to growing your own food as they grow fast and look great as well as being delicious as well as totally versatile in the kitchen.

You will need some seeds and a couple of flat trays, the ones used for propagation.

Fill the trays with soil, tapping them down and level them off. Water the soil well.

Sprinkle the seeds along in rows, about 3 rows to one tray and cover with a thin sprinkling of soil. Water lightly.

It's best to cover these trays with the propagator lids and place them somewhere warm like a window sill while the seeds get going. Once they appear you can take the lid off and let them off. Snip away to your hearts content.

Garlic

Garlic is so easy to grow and very satisfying. Traditionally you should plant your garlic on the shortest day of the year – 21 December – and harvest it on the longest – 21 June.

To grow garlic all you have to do is:

Get some good quality, locally grown garlic from your farmers' market.

Fill a container with soil adding some bits of broken crockery for drainage at the bottom, it needs to be about 25cm deep for the plant and the roots.

Break up your garlic bulb into cloves, leaving the skin on.

Push each clove down into the soil, about 15cm deep and cover them over with more soil, water them in well and leave alone.

Make sure the pot doesn't dry out, you can also plant straight into the ground, they will shoot up quite quickly and benefit from a winter frost.

The bulbs are ready to harvest when the stalks turn yellow and fall over. From the start of July make sure you give the plants plenty of water as this is when they will swell up.

Carefully snuffle your hands down into the soil until you can feel the bulbs and loosen the soil around them, then gently pull them up.

They might be small and they might be big but they are still magic! You can dry the bulbs off on some newspaper on a window sill and then tie them together and hang them up to use in your own time. You can also plant the next batch of garlic from these.

Salad Leaves

Bags of salad cost a lot when you buy enough for a week, you can easily plant a mixture of leaves and snip away all season and feed yourself with delicious, organically grown leaves that you can add to your meals.

Rocket

So called as it grows at lightning speed, fill a tray with compost and sprinkle some seeds over the top, water this and cover with a thin layer of soil, pop on the lid of the tray to generate a hot-house effect and water them lightly every day. If you can sow straight into the ground then do as rocket will return every year with its mad peppery flavour. Mizuna and mustard greens

greens. Chard is a delicious and robust green that's great when just lightly wilted or put in an omelette. It comes in various varieties but the rainbow one is the most exciting one to grow with its bright pink and yellow stems.

Courgettes

These squashes are popular as they are easy to grow and have the most amazing yellow flowers that you can pick and eat, or stuff with ricotta, batter and deep fry. The plants get big and impressive and the fruits taste best when eaten small, about 12cm. Slugs go mad for courgettes, so good luck trying to guard them from these demonic little feckers. Plant the seeds in small pots and plant out the seedlings when they are about 15cm tall and have two true leaves. Plant one to a large tub or give it plenty of space in the ground. Water them well and keep your eyes peeled for slugs. Otherwise they look after themselves.

Pumpkins

Pumpkins are easy to grow, but you need space as they get quite big if you are lucky. They don't fare so well in pots and need lots of manure for really healthy fruits. Start the seeds off in small pots and transfer them outside when they are about 15cm tall and have two 'true' leaves

Tomatoes

A bit of a prima donna but so rewarding when they work out. If you have a deep and tall window sill or glass porch then this is the best place to grow your toms, unless of course you live in the Med or have a polytunnel or greenhouse. I've grown tomatoes outdoors and, in an exceptionally hot Irish summer, they can be amazing. Plant the seeds 2-3 to a small pot/ propagator and water well, cover with a lid and water every two days. When the seedlings are about

can be planted in the same ways as can many 'cut and come again' lettuce varieties. This system works well as you are not waiting for a whole head of lettuce to grow.

Spinach and Chard

Spinach is delicious, but needs space to grow as you need quite a bit of it to make any impact. It is easy to grow however and can be done by following the instructions for rocket, though you will need deeper containers, styroform fish boxes are great for this or even window boxes. Spinach is also a 'cut and come again' plant as is chard so grow these simultaneously for a garden that gives you lots of these important

sweet little gems inside the pea pod, which can be eaten too. Kids go nuts for fresh peas as they are like little green sweets. Make a teepee from some bamboo canes in a large pot filled with soil and plant a pea at the base of each cane. As the shoots grow up, give them some support by tying them loosely to the nearest cane. They will get quite tall with lots of watering and the peas will show themselves and get nice and plump. Don't let them go too far ripening as they will get tough. You can, however, leave some of the pods to dry out on the plant and use the little, ceramic like seeds to grow another crop next year. Grow beans in the same way and just wait for their profusion of beautiful flowers.

Chillis

It's easier to buy a chilli plant from a garden centre and look after it, it will give you gorgeous fruits and save you running out the door and buying one chilli every time you need one.

Potatoes

These fellas that we love so much just love to take their time in the garden. They take up space, so if you don't have much just get yourself a few large shopping bags or potato grow bags – they need to be deep. Seed potatoes are available from January. Just buy what you need. First you 'chit' them by leaving them in open egg boxes on a window sill, green shoots will appear and when these shoots are at least 10cm tall, you can plant them out. Fill your bags about 15cm full with soil and lay the spuds on top of this, about 3 to an average grow bag. Top up the soil, taking care not to cover the tops of the greenery. As the green grows keep topping up the soil. Water regularly or leave them in a rainy spot, still they will need extra watering especially when the flowers appear. When the flowers die off, the spuds are ready to harvest. Few things bring more

5cm tall, thin them out, this means select the strongest plants and plant them on in bigger pots. Tomatoes take a lot of nutrition and will need a big pot each or plant two each in a thick bag of compost lain on its side. Water them well until flowers appear, then pinch off some of the excess side shoots so that all the energy will go into the fruits when they arrive. They will benefit from a feed once a week of potash or nettle tea (see below). You may need to support tall plants with bamboo, cherry varieties don't need this. Allow the fruits to ripen on the plant until you need them.

Peas and Beans

Growing your own peas will give you so many tasty treats from the sprightly pea shoots to the delicious, happiness in the garden than pulling your own potatoes. Have the butter at the ready.

Easy Soft Fruits

Strawberries

It's so easy to grow these delicious fruits. Firstly get your hands on some strawberry plants and plant them into strawberry pots or recycled guttering. Strawberries need to be kept off the soil as the fruits will rot, so it's better to have them in baskets or something similar. Plant them in plenty of compost and keep them watered, or you might get greenfly. The plants will throw out shoots or runners, encourage these by planting them into extra pots of soil while they are still attached to the mother plant, pin them down with some garden wire and cut them off from the Mammy after about two weeks. Cultivated strawberry plants will bear fruit for three years usually but the plants keep on giving. If you can find some alpine strawberries they bear the most incredible tasting tiny fruits and keep going forever,

plant them in cracks in walls or rockeries.

Raspberries

These and they taste amazing compared to shop bought versions. Get some raspberry canes and plant them in big pots in early spring. They spread like crazy in the ground and are quite thorny so it's best to contain them. Water them well and enjoy their delicious soft sweetness.

Foraging

There are so many free foods we can help ourselves to in the town and countryside if we just know what to look for. Elderberries and elderflower are covered in another chapter and blackberries can be gathered in autumn to make delicious jams and desserts. Going out for a walk in spring will show you so many free things we can eat that are great for our health and delicious and full of nutrition, best of all they are free.

Nettles

The wonderous nettle, so misleading, so giving and they make the best feed for your fruiting plants. Pick some hand-fulls of these babies and throw them into a bucket or huge bottle and top it up with water. Leave the whole brew to concoct into the most foul-smelling, stomach churning green goo. Sounds appealing? What nettle tea lacks in finesse it makes up for in nitrogen benefits to the plants you feed with it. Dilute one part to ten and use it to water courgettes, tomatoes and other fruiting plants one a week when they are in fruit.

Nettles can be made into a delicious and blood boosting soup (see p63) or a tea. Be sure to only pick them in April, May or early June as afterwards their nitrogen count is very high. Nettle seeds are often consumed by older folk who swear by their blood-thinning properties.

Dandelion

The leaves are the latest superfood and called a pre-biotic like garlic and onions as they are great for your gut health. You can pick them and eat them raw in a salad or sandwich or wilt them and have them with garlic, spaghetti and olive oil for a cheap, nutritious meal.

Make fritters with dandelion heads when they are yellow by dipping them in batter or sourdough starter and frying them in butter, drizzle with honey for an amazing treat that's full of vitamin C.

Chickweed

This little green grows in any space, crack or pot it can worm its way into. It is full of minerals and has a lovely mild, spicy flavour. Use in salads or the green smoothie on page 39.

Seaweeds

Go seaweed foraging with guidance from a local expert or Prannie Rhatigan's book, *A Seaweed Kitchen*, delicacies like sea spaghetti, dilsik and sugar kelp are delicious, nutritious and free, just waiting to be found. Some 'fucus serratus' wrack with serrated edges is great in a bath for silky smooth skin and a great boost in iodine.

Bibliography

Allen, Darina, *Forgotten Skills of Cooking* (Kyle Cathie Ltd)

Corbin, Pam, *Preserves: River Cottage Handbook No.2* (Bloomsbury)

Katz, Sandor, *Wild Fermentation* (Chelsea Green Publishing Co)

Lawson, Nigella, *How to be a Domestic Goddess* (Random House)

Lawson, Nigella, *Nigella Bites* (Random House)

Ottolenghi, Yotam & Tamimi, Sammi, *Jerusalem* (Ebury Press)

Index